ABC of Criminology

ABC *of* CRIMINOLOGY

ALAIN BAUER

Westphalia Press
An Imprint of the Policy Studies Organization
Washington, DC
2018

Translated by Cadenza Academic Translations
French edition: Les éditions du cerf, 2016

Westphalia Press
An imprint of Policy Studies Organization
1527 New Hampshire Ave., NW
Washington, D.C. 20036
info@ipsonet.org

ISBN-10: 1-63391-678-2
ISBN-13: 978-1-63391-678-4
Cover and interior design by Jeffrey Barnes
jbarnesbook.design

Daniel Gutierrez-Sandoval, Executive Director
PSO and Westphalia Press

Updated material and comments on this edition
can be found at the Westphalia Press website:
www.westphaliapress.org

CONTENTS

Part Two
KEY WORKS

Adler, Freda

Foreword

ALAIN BAUER TAKES A FIRST STEP

In the wake of recent American school shootings, Professor Bauer is spot on with his attention to criminology. He is writing about topics which all of us need to know more about. The need for more considered examination of such topics as gun control, the unsettled relation of mental health to mayhem, the differences between national criminal cultures, education of law enforcement officers, the role of gun control and numerous other topics have been getting intense attention. An updated basic text for the laymen has been lacking, and he provides it.

Some of the proposed solutions, such as arming school teachers or flooding school buildings with smoke underline by their impracticality the need for more rational and academic approaches—which is precisely what this volume sets out to do.

It is an overly optimistic approach to suggest that a single book can solve all the problems that now challenge us. Narcotics alone present enough dilemmas for filling many shelves, let alone the resurgence of kidnaping and slavery, the counterfeiting of technology, and ingenious examples of white collar crime.

What we certainly know is that universities and think tanks have been remiss in the attention being paid by the classroom and curriculum to this long list of issues. The maxim that every journey starts with a single step applies to this ABC.

So this work and one hopes further books from Professor Bauer are witness to the need for an international scholarly approach to an infection of our society which if not challenged can further destabilize democracy. A society where the public safety is challenged as it is today is an endangered society. We must insist that the topics discussed here be given the importance that the current turmoil demands. Kudos to him for his initiatives.

Paul Rich
President, Policy Studies Organization

How to Use This Book

Following a general introduction that provides an epistemological and contextual overview of the topic, the *ABC of Criminology* is divided into two parts:

- Part One, a dictionary of essential concepts, presented in alphabetical order

- Part Two, an anthology of key works from the eighteenth century to the present day, also presented in alphabetical order.

The table of contents is both thematic and analytical, allowing you to move between these two collections in order to read about the concepts in parallel with their use in context.

CRIMINOLOGY WITH A HAMMER

"The necessity of teaching criminology has been unanimously declared by all participants.

This unanimity is unsurprising, since criminology already has a long history as a scientific discipline. Following the works of Cesare Lombroso (1876), Enrico Ferri (1881), and Raffaele Garofalo (1885), it developed through numerous international congresses of criminal anthropology (Rome, 1885; Paris, 1889; Brussels, 1892; Geneva, 1896; Amsterdam, 1901; Turin, 1906; Cologne, 1911). This tradition continued with international congresses of criminology (Rome, 1938; Paris, 1950; London, 1955). However, all sciences are disposed to dissemination through organized teaching.

In fact, at the first International Congress of Criminal Anthropology, Tarde, supported by Enrico Ferri, proposed that students only be admitted to criminal law courses on condition that they first joined a prisoner patronage society and that they took part in weekly visits to prisons, either as groups or individually. In 1890, The Saint Petersburg International Penitentiary Congress expressed a wish 'that a chair of penitentiary science be created in universities.' A similar wish was formulated in 1895 by the Congress of the International Union of Penal Law held in Linz (Austria).

Since then, the idea has frequently been re-expressed. In London, in 1925, the Ninth International Penitentiary Congress affirmed that 'legal training should be complemented by teaching of criminology.' The Third International Congress of Penal Law, the First International Congress of Criminology, and the Twelfth Penal and Penitentiary Congress subsequently expressed similar wishes. Finally, on December 17, 1952, the Meeting of Specialized Agencies and Non-Governmental Organizations Interested in the Prevention of Crime and the Treatment of Offenders, gathered in Geneva under the auspices of the UN, recommended:

1. that universities teach criminology and criminological subjects, according to local traditions, possibilities, and skills.

2. that this teaching be compulsory for those wishing to become judiciary or paralegal professionals;

3. that this teaching have recourse, more widely, to clinical exercises.

Thus, criminology teaching is thought to be necessary not only by criminologists themselves, but by all those involved in preventing crime and treating offenders. In fact, in most countries, there is a surge of opinion demanding a transformation of justice and penal administration. Police, magistrates, and prison staff everywhere feel the need for a change in their methods.

However, in all countries, when they want to act on their good intentions, they find their efforts blocked by a severe or even total lack of norms and precedents. This situation has driven the most determined among them to undertake a difficult task, basing their efforts on practical experience alone, and faced every day with the proof that good will alone can change little. They therefore want scientific training in criminology to be put in place, to help them steer their efforts in the right direction.

They see this training as particularly indispensable since penal and penitentiary reform has created, alongside the traditional auxiliary staff within the penal service (such as medical examiners and psychiatric experts), a new breed of auxiliary staff including psychologists, social workers, and educators. The resultant diversity of legal and paralegal staff makes cohesion difficult to achieve. In order to avoid fragmented work where no-one looks beyond their own domain, shared basic training is required.

Moreover, the evolution of viewpoints, institutions, and staff in the domain of crime prevention and offender treatment poses the question of a renewal of criminal law and procedure. Criminological factors must therefore be taken into account when constructing the rule of law. This means that conventional lawyers must be brought up to date with advances in criminology.

Finally, it should be remembered that beyond professional training for judges and their auxiliaries or for lawyers, criminological teaching is necessary to stimulate scientific research. This research cannot be successful without a constant effort to methodically classify the partial results obtained by individual researchers and integrate them into an overall science, where rigorous systematization allows them to be put in perspective, revealing their full significance. In this approach, training must separate what is confirmed from what is only thought to be true, break down watertight barriers in thinking, draw attention to urgent questions, and disseminate the latest research by various specialists in different countries. To sum up, teaching unifies, co-ordinates, and stimulates scientific research.

These, in brief, are the arguments in favor of teaching criminology. The agreement as to the need for criminological training would have been illusory without discussion regarding the definition of criminology itself.

This problem formed part of the investigation program and was presented to the different reporters. It was also largely addressed in the general introductory note written by one of our group and distributed at the London conference. Similarly, it was addressed at this conference by Mr. Benigno di Tullio, professor at the University of Rome and honorary president of the International Society for Criminology.

The vast majority of participants agreed on Enrico Ferri's conception of criminology as a 'synthetic science' drawing upon criminal anthropology and criminal sociology.

Today, as in the past, the objective of this synthetic science is to reduce criminality and, on the theoretical level that works towards this practical goal, to provide a complete study of the criminal and crime, the latter being viewed not as a judicial abstraction, but as a human action, as a fact of nature and society. The method employed in criminology is that of observation and experimentation, applied within the framework of a true social clinic.

It nevertheless goes without saying that in viewing criminology as a unitary and autonomous science that synthesizes results from clinics and experimentation, the participants at the London conference simply identified a direction—a path to follow. Clearly, this view of criminology supposes that the clinical, experimental approach is sufficiently integrated in practical institutions to allow serious research. The development of observation centers, penitentiary anthropology laboratories, and classification institutes is a prerequisite for the harmonious application of this approach. All were aware that when this condition is not fulfilled or only partially fulfilled, criminology must be content to remain a collection of sciences. It then embraces all those sciences linked to the criminal phenomenon. In these circumstances, it is more appropriate to speak of criminological sciences than of true criminology, since this term applies only to a synthesis of the constituent disciplines.

These two views: criminology as a collection of sciences and criminology as an autonomous science in itself are not mutually exclusive. They are in fact complementary. The social clinic of true criminology uses the methods and data of the fundamental disciplines together. Consequently, the teaching of criminology itself is an extension of, and not a replacement for, the teaching of criminological sciences.

It hardly needs emphasizing that the teaching of criminological subjects and criminology can be usefully complemented by that of related sciences such as legal forensics, scientific policing, and forensic psychology. However, these disciplines should be clearly distinguished from the fundamental disciplines and from criminology itself. Although they study the criminal phenomenon, they do so only to establish the material facts and proof of the crime. They do not envisage scientific study of criminality or seek solutions, whereas this is the precise objective of criminology and the fundamental disciplines.

It is not necessary to insist further on the interest of teaching criminology and on its usefulness for training professionals, students, researchers, and teaching staff.

Essentially, this teaching, as defined above, concerns human criminal activity and aims to assist with the fight against the social ill that is crime. It can thus be perfectly incorporated into social sciences teaching.

When reading various national reports, it is impossible not to be struck by the multiplicity of structures involved in teaching criminology and by the diversity of statuses assigned to it.

One might be tempted to put these differences down to the pluralisms observed in the subject of criminology itself. These fundamental divergences undeniably have some influence at the institutional level. There is, in particular, what can be called an annexing tendency, in which old or traditional disciplines such as penal law consider criminology and the criminological sciences as auxiliary disciplines. This results in an attitude that makes a small space for these disciplines in a pre-established framework unfortunately not designed to accommodate them. The same trend can be seen outside of penal law, and the core disciplines are no exception. Sociology, psychology, biology, and penology all display an annexationist approach to criminology. In fact, the principal factor in the multiplicity of structures for teaching criminology and in the diversity of statuses attributed to it is the variation in the organization of university studies between countries. The contrast is typically made between continental European and Anglo-Saxon universities.

Cambridge University professor M. C. W. Guillebaud emphasized these differences in his remarkable general report on the teaching of economic sciences, which forms the opening to the study of these disciplines in this collection. We will not dwell on the matter here, but it should be noted that his observations are equally applicable to criminology.

These differences in the structure, organization and hierarchy of qualifications between Anglo-Saxon and continental universities have repercussions for university teaching of criminology. The Anglo-Saxon system is less homogeneous than the continental European system, and the United Kingdom system differs from that of the United States (which displays characteristics of both systems). Any brief, general comment on these differences risks being misleading.

Instead, the most important differences for criminology are addressed in the various sections of this report. It is nevertheless possible to make the following preliminary observations:

1. An important difference impacting on the treatment of criminology is that between state and private universities. The tight state control over continental universities and the resultant high uniformity in structure and organization makes for greater uniformity in university teaching of criminology in continental Europe than in the

United Kingdom. Conversely, the autonomy of British private universities, despite the financial aid they receive, allows for greater diversity in exams, programs, and degrees. This naturally creates variation between universities in terms of the importance given to criminology, the number of hours devoted to the subject, the breadth of the topics covered, and the level to which it is taught.

The second consequence of this difference results from it being easier for universities with highly state-controlled administration to provide criminology training for police officers and for penal, probation, or correctional staff. With looser ties between the State and universities, as seen in the UK, the State tends to organize criminological teaching outside of universities for police and correctional staff.

This key difference is clearly visible in the details about training for civil servants found in national reports. Remarkably, there are even differences between Anglo-Saxon countries: The United Kingdom has only private and independent universities, whereas the United States has a mix of state and private universities, so some training colleges for policing and correctional staff are attached to universities, while many others are independent.

2. In general (although wide variation within the system makes generalizations impossible), the Anglo-Saxon system gives less attention to the

subjects often united under the umbrella of criminology (legal forensics, scientific policing, and forensic psychology). Yet this does not imply any disaffection for these subjects. They are simply treated as specialisms and taught accordingly, within lessons devoted to the core disciplines, or in specialist courses offered by institutes or other educational establishments (including teaching organized by the services concerned, for example the police).

3. Another important difference arises from the teaching of sociology being more developed in United States universities and, to a lesser degree, in United Kingdom universities, than in continental Europe. It also arises from the fact that sociology itself has taken a great interest in criminology. This phenomenon has influenced the teaching and direction of criminology, even outside of universities. The discipline is therefore widely taught in sociology departments in the United States and United Kingdom, whereas departments in continental Europe emphasize the links between criminology and law.

   Nevertheless, although specializations are not taught when criminology is taught at a general, elementary level, specialist subjects such as psychiatry and legal forensics are taught as part of the core disciplines in both systems.

4. The hierarchy of university qualifications differs widely between the two systems, but this difference is more a matter of words than of knowl-

edge levels. Nevertheless, Mr. Guillebaud's comments are perfectly applicable to criminology.

5. Many criminology courses exist outside of universities in the United Kingdom and the United States. This complex organization of teaching and the freedom given to educational establishments constitute the two most striking characteristics of the Anglo-Saxon system. These courses either demonstrate the universities' interest in allowing students to audit courses, or are a response to the professional needs of particular groups.

   The in-service training courses for probation officers, the preparatory courses for certain police officer grades, and the courses organized in psychiatric clinics for correctional case workers are all examples of the latter scenario.

   The later sections of this report provide greater detail on this complex teaching structure outside of universities. In general, it can be said that this characteristic of the Anglo-Saxon system aims to provide training that is better adapted to the needs of the professional environment.

6. A further difference between the two systems is that the United Kingdom and United States have highly developed training in social work, with a wide variety of qualifications, diplomas, and certifications. This is particularly visible in criminology teaching in the United Kingdom, where probation officers follow a two-year, full-time university course in order to obtain a social

science diploma, before undertaking more specialist training at the Home Office.

In both countries, many of these courses are not directly linked to criminology, despite having some relationship to it. This trend generally results in improved professional training, producing greater professional competence among the clinical criminologists that are social workers and probation officers.

7. The two systems are deeply entrenched and almost incomparably different. Nevertheless, in both systems, teaching of a multidisciplinary science such as criminology could benefit from the creation of university criminology institutes (naturally, with the appropriate adaptations for each system). This suggestion applies to the Anglo-Saxon as well as the continental system. However, given the current situation in Anglo-Saxon countries, it would have been more logical to distinguish between the criminology taught 'inside' and 'outside' universities rather than that taught 'inside' and 'outside' criminology institutes. This latter classification has nevertheless been retained here to facilitate comparison between various national datasets.

By using this division and by means of this study, we hope to emphasize that each system could benefit from drawing more than they have done so far upon study of the other's respective advantages.

It seems that such study could lead to a greater number of reforms than have been made to date. With this in mind, international exchange of knowledge and experts, encouraged by the International Society for Criminology, can only be beneficial.

Criminology institutes are proposing to unite teaching of criminology, the criminological sciences, and sometimes also criminal law within a single institution. Their organization varies widely: they may be public or private, taking the form of institutes or universities.

As regards their public or private nature, there is quite a clear distinction between Anglo-Saxon institutes and continental European institutes.

Anglo-Saxon institutes are usually private. This is how the Institute for the Study and Treatment of Delinquency, founded in London as a private company in 1931 and initially an open clinic for examining delinquents of all ages, later became an evening school dedicated to social studies, with the fourth year focusing on criminology (these courses depended on the Extra-Mural Department of the University of London and thus on the institution's extension learning service). In the United States, where higher education establishments are too numerous and too diverse for any generalization to be made, it is possible to single out professional development institutes, which target professionals and depend on both the university and the State. One example is the Institute of Correctional Administration, created under the auspices of the General Studies College of George Washington University, which acts as a professional development center for prison and probation service staff.

Although the institute model is not very developed in Anglo-Saxon countries, the same cannot be said of continental countries, where institutes are generally (but not always) public. This is the case in Austria (the Vienna and Graz institutes), Belgium (the criminology departments of the State universities of Ghent and Liège), Brazil (the institute of the Federal District University), France (the Paris and provincial institutes), Italy (the Rome institute), Turkey (the Istanbul and Ankara institutes), and Yugoslavia (the Sarajevo, Ljubljana and Belgrade institutes). All of these are public institutes.

Along with these institutes, the criminology department of the Free University of Leuven and the criminological sciences department of the Free University of Brussels should be mentioned. These are private, but like the institutes listed above, they are university establishments.

The only organized institute existing outside of a university in the continental European countries is the School of Criminology and Technical Policing of the Belgian Ministry of Justice, which is to some extent comparable to American professional development institutes. Almost all of the university institutes are attached to law faculties, with the sole exception of the Stockholm Institute, which since 1947 has been a university institute, while remaining privately funded. This attachment to law faculties has certain consequences. In Paris, the Institute of Criminology is under the scientific direction of the law faculty, the head of its administrative council is the dean of the law faculty, and the director and associate director must be members of the current criminal law teaching body. In Rome, the director is the professor of penal law. In Ljubljana, the director is elected by the law faculty from among its teachers.

Such measures are significant and reveal a lingering juridical imperialism belonging to the old view of criminology as an auxiliary science annexed to or complementing criminal law. One might legitimately wonder whether this juridical preeminence, which once corresponded to a certain historical state of affairs, is now outdated. Criminology supposes a multidisciplinary approach to the individual case and, to judge by the continental countries, its core disciplines belong to the medical and humanities faculties.

In such conditions, it appears that the exclusive attachment of criminology institutes to law faculties might provoke criticisms or reservations from various members of the criminological team. It would therefore be appropriate to bring teaching of criminology within institutes onto neutral grounds, with the 'university institute' model seeming preferable to that of 'institute attached to the law faculty.'

Outside of criminology institutes, the subject is taught in university faculties and establishments linked to scientific research or professional training.

In the Anglo-Saxon countries, criminology is widely taught in university faculties. In the UK, it is linked to the development of social science teaching in universities. The University of London, the London School of Economics (not forgetting the Institute of Psychiatry), and the social sciences faculty at Oxford University seem to have been at the forefront of the movement, followed by numerous universities. At Cambridge, however, criminology is taught within the criminal science department of the law faculties. Elsewhere, it is part of the psychology department (Aberdeen) or the psychological medicine department (Durham).

In the United States, of the 30 most important universities offering graduate training, only five do not teach criminology. In addition to this, 607 colleges (65% of American colleges) offer undergraduate courses in sociology, and criminology is one of the most popular subjects in these courses. This teaching is mostly provided by the sociology or sociology and anthropology departments. Criminology sometimes constitutes a specialist subdivision of the social sciences, while the University of California has a separate criminology department.

In the Anglo-Saxon countries, criminology, in the form of criminal sociology, has thus become closely integrated into the social sciences and sociology departments. This is not the case in continental European countries. Courses in many different faculties undoubtedly evoke 'criminological' problems in passing (psychology and sociology courses within humanities departments, legal forensics and psychiatry courses in medical faculties, or criminal law courses in law faculties). However, core disciplines of criminology are rarely offered individually, exceptions including criminal anthropology in Italy, criminal psychology at the Catholic University in Milan, and forensic psychiatry at Stockholm University. However, many law faculties offer basic teaching more or less complementary to criminal law, under the name 'criminology.' For now, it is sufficient to note the existence of such teaching, as seen at Innsbruck in Austria, at Rio de Janeiro and São Paulo in Brazil, and at Ankara and Istanbul in Turkey. In France, a recent reform introduced a semester of penal law and criminology in the second year of undergraduate law degrees.

Comparable to this university teaching is that provided in certain establishments in connection with scientific research. These establishments and the kinds of teaching they offer are essentially diverse. Sometimes, the research center complements university teaching, as is the case in London, Oxford, and Cambridge. Similarly, in Belgium, the René Marcq Center at the Free University of Brussels provides criminological training for researchers. In France, the School for Advanced Studies provides criminal sociology teaching for researchers and the School of Anthropology (a private institution founded by Broca) offers a criminology course.

Most of the countries studied also offer professional training courses in connection with universities or the various relevant institutions. This model has allowed the University of London and numerous other British universities to organize 'extension' teaching for police and social workers. The Home Office and Scottish Home Department take responsibility for training civil servants working in probation, the police service, the prison service, borstal houses, and approved schools. In Belgium, criminology is taught in nursing and social service schools.

France has a school for prison staff and schools for police and educators, organized by the relevant administrative bodies and teaching rudimentary criminology.

This is also the case in Italy, which has a graduate scientific policing school, as well as a school and professional development courses for social workers. In the United States, teaching for police and penitentiary staff takes place in universities, usually in separate divisions (such as the Berkeley school in California). Teaching is also provided for social workers. Finally, Sweden has an institute for social assistants in Göteborg, offering forensic psychiatry and juvenile criminology courses.

This overview of the structure and status of criminology teaching reveals great disparity. Clearly, this disparity is to some extent an inevitable result of the way things are. However, although it cannot be entirely avoided, it could at least be limited if the model of the university criminology institute already suggested above could be accompanied by centralization and effective coordination of teaching for criminology and the criminological sciences.

The organization of criminology and criminological science teaching presents numerous problems: the conditions for admission, the cost of studies, the number of students, the teaching cycle (duration of studies, exams, and qualifications) and employment prospects.

The access conditions for criminology and criminological science teaching display similar disparity to the structure and status of this teaching.

In the case of criminology institutes, we know that Anglo-Saxon institutes are highly specialist centers. As written by one of our group, their function is the 'multidisciplinary teaching of criminology to people who are already highly trained in one of the related sciences.' The program at the Institute for the Treatment and the Study of Delinquency in London includes courses aimed at specialists, while also providing for the learning needs of non-specialists. In the United States, prior professional selection is used in admission procedures for the specialist institutes, because of the limited number of places. This explains why the model is one of professional development schools. In Belgium, the School of Criminology and Technical Policing of the Ministry of Justice is reserved for magistrates, lawyers, university graduates, and those with specialist knowledge.

In continental European criminology institutes attached to law faculties, there are two models for entry conditions. In the first, institute courses in criminology, the criminological sciences, and related sciences form an ensemble and must all be studied together. Criminology teaching is consequently independent of the law program. It is an additional course with particular entry requirements. In the second model, however, courses at the criminology institute do not form an ensemble. Law students simply have to follow one of the courses during their studies.

When teaching at a criminology institute is compulsory and complementary, proof of prior scientific training is an admission requirement. The Leuven criminology school in Belgium accepts applicants holding an 'applicant' university degree and medical students having successfully completed the second year, which serves as an 'application' test in the natural and medical sciences. Similar conditions apply in Brussels, Ghent, and Liège. In Paris, only students with at least a Bachelors in law or holding a certificate of legal competence are admitted, together with students in the humanities, science, or medicine. In Rome, graduates in law, economy, commerce, or the political and social sciences, and medical doctors or surgeons, as well as those holding a degree from another university, can register. In Turkey and Yugoslavia, admission depends on academic and professional qualifications.

It can thus be seen that when a criminology institute provides compulsory or additional teaching, the entry conditions range from those applied to ordinary higher education applicants (as in Belgium), to conditions similar to those required by Anglo-Saxon style professional development institutes (as in Rome, Turkey, and Yugoslavia), with a variety of intermediary situations (as in Paris). The same does not apply when one of the programs is compulsory for law students (Vienna, Graz): they must take two hours of criminology per week for one semester. It should also be noted that students in other faculties can attend the institute's courses. Auditing is also allowed on these courses.

Given these admission requirements, it is remarkable that no establishment asks applicants to take a preparatory course teaching the basics of biology, psychology, and sociology—notions without which it would seemingly be very difficult to follow anything more than a rudimentary course. General or specialist university qualifications or even professional experience in particular areas cannot be a substitute for the rational acquisition of this basic knowledge.

Criminological teaching outside of institutes is less problematic in terms of entry conditions. In the United Kingdom, where criminology is most often taught as a branch of the social sciences, it is obviously the entry conditions for these studies that count. Similarly, in the United States, all sociology or social administration students have the opportunity to follow the general criminology modules in universities. In the Anglo-Saxon countries, the criminological sciences are also taught outside of sociology departments, as a part of the general teaching of the other core disciplines. In continental Europe, specialized teaching in the core disciplines (criminal anthropology, criminal psychology, forensic psychiatry), where it exists, takes place within the framework of corresponding studies in medicine and psychology. Notions of criminology within or linked to criminal law are reserved for law students. The same applies for humanities or medical students, when criminological notions are evoked in relation to other courses in their programs (such as psychology, sociology, psychiatry, or forensics)."

These words might be taken for plagiarism, if I did not immediately hold up my hands and confess it. For this text is in no way new. It dates from 1956, and was written by Denis Carroll and Jean Pinatel for the UNESCO Congress on Criminology. This congress took place in Paris. Criminology has developed everywhere. Everywhere except, for a very long time, in France.

In fact, since the 1950s, academic pressures have ceaselessly pitched disciplinary monopolies against criminology's fight to be recognized as a scientific discipline. Criminology is essentially just one in a long line of disciplines defending its turf as part of a struggle for recognition. Yet these other struggles have been rapidly forgotten.

Criminology is not in fact the only discipline to have suffered. Before it, the oriental languages (under Francis I of France), the sciences and technologies, economics and management (during the French Revolution), political science (during the Second Empire) and many other disciplines including penal law, environmentalism, and journalism were not accepted by the old Sorbonne. Not to mention the "schools" of psychology and economics. The situation is, unfortunately, nothing new.

One might think that Emile Durkheim himself would have been able to resolve this somewhat hazy controversy:

> [...] We observe that certain actions exist which all possess the one external characteristic that, once they have taken place, they provoke on the part of society that special reaction known as punishment. We constitute them as a group sui generis and classify them under a single heading: any action that is punished is termed a crime and we make crime, so defined, the subject matter of a special science of criminology.
>
> —Emile Durkheim, *The Rules of Sociological Method,* trans. Steven Lukes (New York: The Free Press, 1982)

Others have also made determined and equally worthy efforts to define criminology: Jacques Léauté, in *Criminologie et Science Pénitentiaire* (Paris: PUF, 1972), states that "[t]he aim of criminology is the scientific study of the whole criminal phenomenon," while Gaston Stefani,

Georges Levasseur, and Roger JambuMerlin, in a work of the same title, *Criminologie et Science Pénitentiaire* (Paris: Dalloz, 5th ed. 1982), state that "[t]he criminological sciences are those that study delinquency in order to look for its causes, its origins, its processes and consequences." In *Criminologie* (Paris: Dalloz, 6th ed. 2007), Raymond Gassin defines it as:

> [...] the science that studies the factors and processes of criminal action and which determines, using knowledge of these factors and processes, the best means of combat to contain and if possible reduce this social ill.

Henri Ellenberger's definition in *Criminologie du Passé et du Présent* (Montreal: Presses de l'Université de Montréal, 1966), is as follows: "[...] Alongside the general sciences, criminology belongs to the complex sciences, and like them it is recognizable by the following characteristics:

1. [It is] located at a crossroads with sciences from which [...] it remains separate, but to which it is related [...];

2. It is not purely theoretical, and is given meaning only by its practical application [...];

3. It is neither entirely general nor entirely specific, but rather it constantly moves back and forth from general to specific, specific to general [...];

4. It works not only with scientific concepts but also with concepts expressing value judgments [...];

5. It is characterized by an independent ethical goal: To prevent crime, rather than have to punish it. If punishment is necessary, the minimum effective punishment should be used, and reeducation should be combined with the punishment [...]

Robert Cario also proposes a definition in his *Introduction aux Sciences Criminelles* (Paris: L'Harmattan, 6th ed. 2008):

> Criminology can be defined as a multidisciplinary science whose objective is the global and integrated analysis of the social phenomenon caused by criminal actions, in their origins and their dynamics, in their individual and social dimensions, from the viewpoint of the perpetrator as well as that of the victim, for goals of prevention and treatment.

One might believe that this avalanche would have been enough to stem the sociolatry whose denial of reality constituted at once its charm, its difference and its fundamentalism, particularly in France ... and only in France .... For, as discussed with colleagues in a recent opinion piece,[1] a discipline is above all a political fact whose scientific scope must integrate recognition in order to reestablish its goals. The autonomy of penal law, the birth of the criminal sciences, and recognition of the very notion of criminal policies had to be argued politically, as did the free practice of teaching clinical psychology and

---

1   Loïck-M. Villerbu, Robert Cario, Martine Herzog-Evans, and Alan Bauer, "La criminologie estelle une science?," *Cahiers Français* 372 (January 2013).

sociology in the universities. The fact that contemporary criminal lawyers have chosen to write a treatise on penal law and criminology[2] clearly shows that the two cannot be thought of as the same discipline, just as criminology cannot be reduced to the criminal sciences, even if they are accompanied by sociological considerations and psychological or psychiatric humanism.[3]

Although criminology has been taught in France, it has had no official university recognition, in that there was no qualification for it before the creation of the Chair of Criminology at the Conservatoire National des Arts et Métiers in 2010 and its Master's degree in Forensic Sciences and Criminology. Until then, and still too often now, it was merely an add-on whose disciplinary avatars were weak. It therefore took refuge at worst in private institutions, at best in university degrees or interuniversity degrees. The number of these had continued to rise, reaching 130 in 2010. Hence the words used by members of the French National Criminology Commission in the November 2009 Villerbu Report[4] to designate both studies of criminology and those that benefited

2   Gaston Stefani and Georges Levasseur, *Droit Pénal Général et Criminologie* (Paris: Dalloz, 1957); Robert Vouin and Jacques Léauté, *Droit Pénal et Criminologie* (Paris: PUF, 1956). See also Pierre Bouzat and Jean Pinatel, *Traité de Droit Pénal et de Criminologie* (Paris: Dalloz, 1970).

3   When dealing with the relationship of *crime* (a judicial formulation) to *criminal* (the person responsible for the crime), these take the names of criminal psychology, criminal psychiatry, and criminal sociology.

4   Loïck-M Villerbu, Report by the Minister of Higher Education and Research, on the Feasibility, Creation and Development of Criminology Studies, Research and Training (Villerbu Report). Presented by the French National Criminology Commission, 2010.

from it as "homeless" and "paperless," even while the media constantly promotes criminological information that is often partial in both senses of the word, prioritizing the scoop over educational value.[5] It should further be emphasized that criminological thought then formed part of the teaching of over 110 university academics and interested many practical stakeholders, despite the fact that work in criminology severely lacked visibility.

The French paradox arises from these points: since emerging at the end of the nineteenth century at the crossroads between four recognized disciplines (forensic medicine, psychiatry/mental health, law, sociology), criminology remained an accessory to penal law, which is simply a long-ignored component of private law. Its legitimacy as an academic and social discipline comes in a context of institutional deficiency. It seems that systematic or systemic analysis is not appropriate for studying the criminal phenomenon: criminology tends to rely on texts, doctrine, case-law,[6] or the multiple theories in the humanities and the social, economic, or political sciences. When the observations are practical, we see a return to their disciplinary origin, even if this is highly disputed: can psychiatry really be a way of understanding all criminal behavior? Does sociology have all the answers? Can psychology be sure of the origin of criminal ideas and acts, of the victim's position etc., when their fragmentation necessitates a selective vision if totalitarianism is to be avoided?[7]

---

5   No news item would be complete without an interview from a self-proclaimed criminologist.

6   See Bernard Bouloc, *Pénologie* (Paris: Dalloz, 1991).

7   See Eric Heilmann, ed., *Science ou Justice: Les Savants, l'Ordre et la Loi* (Paris: Autrement, 1994).

Because criminology in France is seen as a specialism and not as a discipline, the effects of norms and changes to norms give little occasion for study that might enrich the perspectives of public policies for the territory or the city in question. The discipline thus gives little attention to collective criminality (organized crime and terrorism), to transnational criminality (cartels and mafias), to forms of criminality attributable to the state of the modern world (the "dark side" of globalization), or to the development of criminal networks with the opening up of markets, the development of new technologies, and new forms of consumerism.

The National Criminology Commission, which benefited from the presence of professionals in the field and analyzed observations by representatives of diverse origins and opinions in an attempt to end the clandestine practices of members and partial institutions,[8] submitted its conclusions in July 2011. The report only began to pose problems for some when, after a number of reformulations and conditions, it came to creating a criminology department with the aim of allowing the academics concerned to build a clear university career. The decree creating such a section within the National Council of Universities was courageously published in the *Journal Officiel* on March 15, 2012, by minister Wauquiez but was repealed in August of the same year, due to a change in the political majority. Over a hundred academics made their feelings known in regard to the situation. More than in certain existing sections ...

---

8   These clandestine practices are costly: the partisans of existing disciplines ensure that many criminology teaching jobs go to pre-selected or inside candidates, and many teachers expressing an interest in criminology are passed over for promotion.

France's National Criminology Commission aimed to make general and integrated research in the undergraduate, masters, and doctoral systems possible and to guarantee democratic access for all (not currently the situation in private or even public university programs).[9] Initial, specialized, or ongoing training for teachers, researchers, and professionals in the penal system or generally involved in dealing with crimes committed or suffered would ideally guarantee scientific content based on an ethic of independence and freedom of the universities, as required by the traditional deontology of university personnel and by the pedagogical imperatives that they follow. In the words of Edgar Morin and Stéphane Hessel, these considerations are typical "of a love of the knowledge delivered and the people that it is delivered to."[10]

There are three easily identifiable levels of criminological intervention. The first is prevention programs for all forms of vulnerability, corresponding to various professions, which aim to reduce the risk factors affecting vulnerable children and adolescents. These programs aim to strengthen protection measures and enable harmonious (re)integration. The second, when prevention fails, is intervention throughout the penal process by professionals with critical knowledge based on experience and exposure to research. Their knowledge areas range from the effects of violent acts to those of past violence, as seen in secondary victimization.[11] The third consists of

---

9   Villerbu Report, 3962.

10   Edgar Morin and Stéphane Hessel, *Le Chemin de l'Espérance* (Paris: Éditions Fayard, 2011), 2021.

11   Secondary victimization is when a person re-lives their trauma upon the occurrence of a new event that may or may not be linked to the initial trauma.

ways of dealing with crime and its perpetrators, which result, as far as possible, in recognition of guilt. Developing the skills of those who deal with convicted criminals would encourage criminals to "desist"[12] (stop reoffending). These skills go beyond the social, economic, or psychological factors of rehabilitation that are traditionally seen as factors in ending delinquency. Developments of this kind have led to remarkable creations of "therapeutic jurisprudence"[13] in the United States, or of jurisdictions that resolve the problem at hand.

However, this kind of intervention will remain a pious wish unless independent, scientific, regular, and sustained solutions are applied.

There have been numerous criticisms of the new criminology university section. Although "contestation is a necessary condition for renewal of a science,"[14] objections are all too often based on unfounded common opinion and illegitimate reductionism. Security-based ideology,[15]

12　See, for example, Fergus McNeill, Peter Raynor, and Chris Trotter, *Offender Supervision: New Directions in Theory, Research and Practice*, (London: Willan Publishing, 2010).

13　Martine Herzog-Evans, "Révolutionner la pratique judiciaire: S'inspirer de l'inventivité américaine," *Recueil Dalloz* 44 (January 2012): 30163022.

14　Georges Kellens, "Interactionnisme versus personnalité criminelle," in *Les Grandes Tendances de la Criminologie Contemporaine* (Proceedings of the 7th International Criminology Congress of Belgrade, 1973). Institut des Recherches Criminologiques et Sociales, Vol. 1, 1980, 118-128.

15　Nathalie Brafman and Isabelle Rey-Lefebvre, "La criminologie érigée en discipline autonome," *Le Monde*, March 13, 2012; Damien Helene, "La criminologie: nouvelle discipline universitaire en France," *France Soir*, March 16, 2012; Motion carried on March 21, 2012 by the permanent Commission of the National Council of Universities (CPCNU); H. Tassel, "La criminologie personal criticisms,[16] and worries about the instrumentalization of universities[17] discredit the objections, unless it is to be considered that scientific disciplines, autonomous or otherwise, necessarily belong to current political thought, even if their applications are universal.

We should expect criminology to address the suffering of victims in a practical, humane, restorative, and therapeutic manner, as well as a scientifically enlightened and well-founded one. Those adhering to certain currents of thought are generally uncomfortable with victims,[18] since they focus—as do I—on the criminals. Victims are therefore seen as an obstacle to dealing with offenders.[19]

à l'université? Fuite en avant, imposture scientifique et désinvolture ...," March 23, 2012. http://humanite.fr; Laurent Mucchielli, Olivier Nay, Xavier Pin, and Daniel Zagury, "La 'criminologie' entre succès médiatique et rejet universitaire," *Le Monde*, March 29, 2012; "Création d'une Section du CNU 'criminologie': non à la Section 'Guéant'," April 4, 2012, http://ferc-sup.cgt.fr.

16 See Laurent Mucchielli "Une 'nouvelle criminologie française': Pour qui et pour quoi?" *Revue de Science Criminelle et de Droit Pénal Comparé*, October/December 2008, 795-803; Laurent Mucchielli, "Vers une criminologie d'État en France? Institutions, acteurs et doctrines d'une nouvelle science policière," *Politix* 89 (2010): 195-214; Laurent Mucchielli, "La 'criminology' en France et ses arrière-plans idéologiques," March 20, 2011. http://laurent-mucchielli.org; Ruling creating a criminology section published in the *Journal Officiel*, March 15, 2012. http://vousnousils.fr).

17 See "Non à la 75è section," http://petition24.net; "Déclaration des présidents du Conseil scientifique et du Conseil des formations du CNAM," April 4, 2012; Virginie Gautron, Laurent Leturmy, Christian Mouhanna, and Laurent Mucchielli, "Criminologie en France (suite): pour un moratoire total sur les projets actuels," March 15, 2011, http://laurent-mucchielli.org.

18 Relevant here is the experience described in Dominique Lemarchal, "La victime et son autre," *AJ Pénal* (2008): 349351.

19 Robert Cario, "Qui a peur des victimes?," *AJ Pénal*, no.12 (2004): 434437.

Does this mean that these researchers are incapable of feeling equal empathy for the offenders and the victims, or is it because consideration of victims casts doubt on current penal arrangements?

It should be noted that even early criminologists, albeit only in passing, drew attention in their work to the necessary consideration of the victim within the penal response to the criminal act. Thus, founders of criminology such as Enrico Ferri thought that remedying the harm to victims of criminal acts was a necessary objective of punishment.

These considerations led France's National Criminology Commission to state that "criminology is 'the scientific study of the criminal phenomenon and the responses that are applied or may be applied by society,' taking into account penal flaws, deviations and contraventions. It has a triple objective: prevention, control, and treatment. Current public policy is used to provide a context and perspective for study. Each of the three objectives gives rise to its own research path and content: prevention may be primary, secondary or tertiary; control involves identifying, characterizing and stopping the criminal and the consequences of crime (the procedures, the forensic, psychiatric and psychological examinations, the alternatives to prosecution); treatment poses questions regarding the rights of parties, help for victims, reintegration or rehabilitation, restorative responses, compensation or mediation. These research paths require experienced and 'certified' specialists."

Over 120 years after Durkheim, and 60 years after the Paris Congress, with criminology now also being taught in France, albeit in an official capacity only at the Conservatoire National des Arts et Métiers, it is becoming an emerging discipline. It no longer needs scientific justification or concrete acknowledgement. What it needs now is to mobilize society.

In this new phase of development, it is necessary to finally provide an ABC of the main authors with an overview of the major concepts in criminology. Here is that ABC.

Alain Bauer

Professor and chair of Criminology at the Conservatoire National des Arts et Métiers (since 2009), director of the Master's degree in Criminology, academic director and vice-chair of the academic council of the defense and security council of the Conservatoire National des Arts et Métiers.

Associate professor at Fudan University in Shanghai.

Professor and chair of Forensic and Criminal Sciences for the Specialized MBA in Security Management of the French National Gendarmerie

Senior research fellow at the Center of Terrorism, John Jay College of Criminal Justice in New York (United States) and the Chinese University of Law and Political Science in Beijing.

Editor of the *International Journal on Criminology,* member of the editorial board of *PRISM* (National Defense University, Washington), and member of the academic commitee of the *Revue Française de Criminologie et de Droit Pénal* (Paris)

Part One

CONCEPTS

Anomie

The concept of anomie was introduced by Émile Durkheim in *The Division of Labor in Society*, and revisited in *Suicide*. Durkheim highlights the importance of social norms in regulating individual goals and the methods of pursuing them. Anomie is a situation in which these standards are found to be weak and unable to fulfill their role, so that society is no longer able to maintain the cultural codes necessary for it to function. The elimination of the value system makes relations unstable, introduces strain, and provokes conflict.

In his article "Social Structure and Anomie," published in 1938, Robert Merton took up Durkheim's idea to make anomie a central concept in his analysis of American society. Merton makes a distinction between two elements: the cultural structure, which represents the values around the goals to be achieved and the methods of achieving these goals, and the social structure, which relates to social relationships and positions. In a balanced society, these structures are integrated—but disjunction can occur. Thus, in Merton's view, American society overvalues goals to such an extent that succeeding (the American dream) becomes more important than following the rules, and this leads to the search for other means of achievement, either through innovation, or through crime. This devaluation of standard methods leads to an initial state of anomie. In addition, there are social inequalities in American society that limit the access of some individuals to the means of success, thus creating strain and favoring recourse to illegal means. This is the second form of anomie. These situations, above simple social disorganization, create tensions and conflicts conducive to criminal behavior.

Merton's analysis of anomie involves the role of "strain," or tension, and this particular dimension was subsequently developed in the various models of strain theory.

Merton sought to make sense of the strains interwoven into American society, and in their 1994 work *Crime and the American Dream*, Steven Messner and Richard Rosenfeld extended this analysis by developing institutional anomie theory. Like Merton, Messner and Rosenfeld propose that while the American dream places strong emphasis on material and financial success, it is less concerned with the means of achieving this. They believe that the cultural importance accorded to money also penetrates all sectors of society, so that non-economic ends, such as family or education, are devalued through submission to the logic of economy. These institutions suddenly lose their ability for socialization and thus facilitate the creation of an institutional anomie.

Biopsychology

One of the routes taken in the biologizing approach to criminals has been consideration of the somatic and psychological characteristics that lead to the development of "constitutions" or "types."

In the early twentieth century the theory of degeneration was on the decline, and alienist Ernest Dupré, who had developed the concept of mythomania, proposed a new explanation: "constitutional perversity" (*Les Perversions Instinctives*, 1912). For Dupré, perversity has a neurophysiological basis, and results from pathological and congenital dysfunction. Dupré recognizes three instincts: reproduction, conservation, and association. The instinct of association, which characterizes the social being, develops later than the two instincts of conservation and procreation, which are the most primitive and will win out in the event of conflict. In this sense the perversion of the instinct of association, which produces offenders, is not therefore moral indifference but the inversion of altruism, the perverse desire to make fellow beings suffer.

Dupré's work opened up an avenue that would be revisited and expanded throughout the twentieth century. Milestones in this field include Ernst Kretschmer's 1925 classification of different physical types, Olof Kinberg's research in 1935, Earnest Albert Hooton's 1939 racial classification, William Herbert Sheldon's somatotype taxonomy in 1940 and his list of different physical types, which influenced the Gluecks, and Benigno Di Tullio's 1951 theory of delinquent constitution, which proposed a set of physical and mental predispositions for crime.

Finally, in his 1964 work *Crime and Personality*, Hans Jürgen Eysenck broke down personalities into three dimensions: extraversion (impulsive tendencies), neuroticism (anxiety, emotional instability), and psychoticism (isolation, aggression, lack of empathy). Higher levels of these three dimensions, which Eysenck saw as being biological in nature, might affect the social conditioning process and enable criminal behavior to develop.

Biosocial theories

These theories are based on the principle that all human actions are the result of interactions between individual predispositions and the environment. They thus advocate taking biological data into account when considering a crime, while recognizing the importance of the social environment—hence the name "biosocial." These new movements have, however, experienced resistance from the dominant sociological tradition which, on principle, excludes such determinations, and the use of research from fields such as genetics, neurosciences, and evolutionary biology, has reawakened the ghosts of racism and eugenics. The biosocial approach does not however seek to make sense of crime, which is an event, but of criminality. It can be divided into three approaches, based on genetics, evolutionary theory, or the neurohormonal sciences, none of which seek to establish determinants, but rather the tendency to respond in a certain way in a given environment. Since crime is committed by individuals, it is important to reintroduce the individual factor into structural data in order to produce a more precise picture of the criminal act. This is a predictive, non-explanatory approach.

Broken windows theory

When it comes to crime, the justice system always in-
tervenes in a reactive manner, once the offense has been
committed. But crime can be approached differently,
seeking to prevent rather than punish, by acting to reduce opportunities or temptation.

In 1982, James Q. Wilson and George L. Kelling published their article "Broken Windows." The authors start-
ed from the principle that a neighborhood can become
an at-risk area through a three-stage process. First, there
is uncivil behavior. Such behavior is not criminal, but it
drives "civil" people to leave the neighborhood, leaving
public spaces to be taken over by uncivil populations
in the second stage of the process. From then on, the
neighborhood is prey to offenders, who believe they can
operate there with impunity. This is illustrated by the
metaphor of the broken window. If a broken window
on a house is not repaired, the negligence signals that
nobody cares about what is happening there. Breaking
a window has no consequences. But if one window is
not repaired, very quickly other windows will be broken,
so this situation, this sign of abandonment, leads to di-
sastrous consequences. This approach sees crime not as
caused by phenomena such as poverty or inequality, but
as due to a breach of morality. To prevent it, the solution
is therefore a vigorous response to minor offenses in dis-
organized areas, a strategy which through some misunderstanding has come to be identified with a policy of
"zero tolerance." The authors of "Broken Windows" certainly envisaged zero tolerance to incivility, but through
methods other than penal repression, while the policy of
"zero tolerance" has proceeded from the opposite end of

the spectrum through the penalization of incivility, and has been condemned most notably by George Kelling himself.

Cartography/Geography

Cartography and geography have never been far from criminology. Although these fields initially focused on large territories—countries, cities, and neighborhoods—they now focus on more specific places such as local sites and addresses.

André-Michel Guerry was the first criminologist not only to make use of statistical analysis, but also to plot crime and draw up a national crime map, and the Chicago School (Robert Ezra Park and Ernest Burgess in particular) later closely linked the urban geography of large American cities to the phenomenon of crime. Within the city space, research then focused on particular areas (Clifford Shaw and Henry McKay) and specific neighborhoods.

During the 1970s and early 1980s, following studies such as George Kelling's 1973 report on "The Kansas City Preventive Patrol Experiment," there was a reconsideration of policing on the ground, and criminologists also shifted focus from the causes to the material conditions of crime. As a result, the geographic approach moved from revealing the distribution of crime to focusing on spaces themselves as a dimension of the criminal act. In 1979, Marcus Felson called for the physical site of crime to be considered as a determining factor, and in 1983 Ronald V. Clarke published his research into situational crime prevention, in which the layout of place is also a determining element. In his 1989 article "Hot Spots of Crime and Criminal Careers of Places," Lawrence W. Sherman observes that crimes are concentrated in a number of hot spots and that it is easier to predict where crime will take place than who will commit it. Finally, in 1991, Paul and Patricia Brantingham's *Environmental Criminology* introduced design, as place and spatial configuration, as a factor in the criminal act.

Chicago School

In the early twentieth century the Department of Sociology at the University of Chicago became the center of research into crime and deviance. It began by researching urban areas and urban ecology. In 1925 Robert Ezra Park, Ernest Burgess, Louis Wirth, and Roderick McKenzie published *The City*, a collection of articles presenting research on Chicago, which was growing exponentially and experiencing a number of issues, particularly in relation to the integration of immigrant populations. Early empirical studies showed a higher crime rate in the poorest area, which had the worst sanitation and social conditions; they also showed that this rate remained stable over many years regardless of the population flux in this area. Criminality thus appeared to be linked to urban and social conditions, independently of individuals, and researchers argued that crime analysis should therefore abandon the criminal personality approach, which dominated positivist criminology, and adopt a sociological approach, identifying the causes of crime in factors such as disorganization, cultural conflict, strain, and the environment. The Chicago School, a broad church for various theories and theorists (including Clifford Shaw, Henry McKay, Thorsten Sellin, Edwin Sutherland, and Albert K. Cohen), who nevertheless shared the same approach, had a significant impact on criminology in the Anglo-Saxon countries.

Conflict theory

There are two opposing perspectives when it comes to evaluating society and crime. There are those for whom society is founded on a general consensus through which the state brings together the various groups of which it is composed, and for whom the criminal act is an identifiable breach of shared values. In contrast, there are those who see society as a place of conflict in which the state represents the interests and values of the groups who are able to control it. In this view, individuals are more likely to become criminals if they are part of a group that is excluded or kept away from power.

Although various conflict theories have been proposed, they all have three elements in common. First, the relative nature of the definition of crime. No act is intrinsically criminal, but rather an act is defined, or labeled as criminal, based on the interests prevailing in the society. As interests change, so will the definition. Second, the view that certain interests have control of the major institutions (including laws, religion, education, and the economy) and are thus able to remain dominant. And finally, the idea that the law is an instrument of power.

The importance of cultural conflict was recognized by the Chicago School in its work on the problems posed by immigration, but it was Thorsten Sellin who introduced conflict theory into criminology. In his 1938 work *Culture Conflict and Crime*, Sellin highlights the fact that complex societies are societies in conflict. He makes a distinction between primary cultural conflicts, when two or more cultures clash within the same society (colonialism or immigration, for example), and secondary cultural conflicts, when a society develops into multiple subcultures. In these circumstances, the law represents the norms of the dominant culture, normality, and if the norms it defends come into conflict with the norms of a secondary culture, the latter will appear to be deviant. In 1955, Albert Cohen modified Sellin's theory by linking juvenile delinquency to an adolescent subculture, arguing that conflict did not take place between the dominant norms and those of a minority social group, but between the dominant norms and the adolescent subculture.

This approach was later revisited from a structural rather than cultural perspective toward the end of the 1950s, when George Vold (*Theoretical Criminology*, 1958), based on the principle that men act in and through groups, envisaged society, and criminality, as a space of conflict opposing multiple groups pursuing different goals. In the 1960s and 1970s, Marxist-inspired theories took up the idea of conflict, interpreting it in terms of class, while others developed Vold's pluralist perspective. All shared a shift in focus from the question "Why do certain people commit crimes?" to "Why are certain acts defined as criminal?"

Crime

Crime can be narrowly defined as an offense, an act punished by the law, or more broadly as the transgression of a norm. In the first case the perspective is legal, and in the second it is sociological, a view in which crime is simply a subsection of the category of deviance.

In the legal definition, it is the law that endows certain types of behavior with a specifically criminal nature, and which draws the map of crime by defining what is licit and illicit. But the law is linked to the cultural and historical contexts that have produced it: it varies across time and place, and thus so does the definition of crime. There is also the question of the legislator, a particular focus of critical criminology. Yet a definition of crime seeking to free itself from the limits of the law by considering only the transgression of a norm comes up against similar problems, for norms are equally relative and, as with the law, there remains the issue of who establishes them. The consensual approach supposes that there is a majority view on the definition of what constitutes norms, and therefore crime as their transgression. But the conflictual approach, which envisages society as a site of conflict between different groups, views the norms in force as the expression of a particular group with the ability to impose them.

In the field of criminology, theories can be classified into two broad groups. On one hand, there are the theories that consider crime primarily from the angle of its legal definition, asking questions such as why a particular type of behavior is criminalized, who makes such a decision, and how society responds. On the other hand, and more numerous, there are the theories that focus on the socio-logical dimension, and consider the transgression of the norm in its social dimension. They seek to make sense of individual and group deviance, and ask questions such as why a certain section of society, or a certain environment, has a higher crime rate than another.

Criminal

Like crime, a criminal can be defined in a strictly legal sense, as someone who is convicted of breaking the law. A broader scope might, however, in line with classical criminology, consider a criminal to be an ordinary, free man, who makes choices, in which case there is nothing particular to say about him. Or we might, through the sociological lens, continue to consider him as an ordinary man, but one subject to socioeconomic pressures, in which case the focus moves away from the criminal himself to consider the socioeconomic processes that lead to crime. Finally, in line with the positivist school of criminology, we can consider the criminal as a particular individual. Taking the criminal into consideration can be understood in two ways: either the *criminal* is considered as a "natural," biological being, a particular species within the human genus, or *the* criminal is considered, the individual, psychological profile involved in the crime, as an element of it. The former approach applies to Lombroso, with his "born criminal" and various types of criminal constitution. The latter is a contemporary approach that rejects determinism but nevertheless holds that the offender should be reintroduced into our understanding of crime.

Criminal anthropology

Criminal anthropology is generally considered to be the early name of what would become "criminology." In truth, however, "criminal anthropology" was initially concerned with the anatomical, biological, and sociological characteristics of criminals (a broad scope that Paul Topinard sought to amend by calling for the term criminal anthropology to be reserved for research into biology and for the term criminal sociology to be created for research into social conditions), while "criminology" was concerned with the legal study of the crime, or more precisely the legal consequences that should result from new understanding of criminals (it was in this sense that Raffaele Garofalo initially conceived of the term).

In France, criminal anthropology was particularly associated with the Lyon School and Alexandre Lacassagne's "Archives of Criminal Anthropology." This school was characterized by rejection of Lombroso's "born criminal" concept and an emphasis on the environmental setting, but remained profoundly influenced by the positivism of the era, and drew partly on Gall's theory of phrenology. Consideration of the environment—which stemmed from the neo-Lamarckism of the French school compared to the Darwinism of the Italian school—was combined with anatomical and biological data derived from medicine. For the Lyon school, crime was not the consequence of an atavism or innate predisposition, but resulted from the interaction between individuals and their environment.

With the decline of both the Lyon school and the theories of Lombroso's Italian school, the term criminal anthropology gave way to that of criminology, which better reflected the contribution made by the humanities to criminal law.

Criminalistics

The term criminalistics, or forensic science, refers to the set of techniques used to identify the causes and circumstances of a crime as well as the perpetrator. The term was invented by Austrian researcher Hans Gross in his 1893 book *Kriminalistik*, and "criminalistique" was first used in French by Edmond Locard in 1912 to refer to the laboratories charged with assisting investigations by analyzing traces from crime scenes.

By this point, the development of criminalistic techniques was already well advanced. Francis Galton's *Finger Prints* had been published in 1892, and his technique of identification through fingerprints was being used by the police service; while from 1879 onwards Alphonse Bertillon had been developing his technique of anthropometry. Anthropometric identification, or "Bertillonage," consisted of various physical measurements designed to identify repeat offenders, and Bertillon also developed offender mug shots and measured crime scene photography, other techniques that were already largely in widespread use. In addition to these methods of identification, police services had also developed various techniques for interpreting the material evidence left at the crime scene. In 1909, Rodolphe Archibald Reiss founded the Institute of Forensic Science at the University of Lausanne and finally, in 1910, Edmond Locard himself had opened a forensic science laboratory in Lyon.

Since then, many types of laboratory have developed around different specialties—including physics, chemistry, biology, finance, and computing—organized around the various sectors and methods of crime.

Criminology

"Criminology" emerged as a science during the nineteenth century. Initially known under various other names, including criminal anthropology, it settled around the end of the nineteenth century under the heading of criminology. The origin of the term is disputed. Some attribute it to Raffaele Garofalo, in 1885, and others to Paul Topinard, in 1887.

Criminology is a complex discipline precisely because its subject is complex, and tackling it requires contributions from many different specialties—including legal science, sociology, and psychology—which has led to its own status as a science being contested.

In his work *Principles of Criminology*, Edwin Sutherland follows Ernest Burgess in distinguishing three approaches to crime: a) the law, and the conditions presiding over its development; b) transgression, and the search for the causes of crime; and c) the response to the crime. These three directions provide a rough map of the fields within criminology.

Like any discipline, criminology has a history. It began with the so-called *classical criminology* of the Enlightenment, which emphasized freedom of choice. During the nineteenth century this gave way to *positivist criminology*, which sought to establish its scientific foundations, arguing that crime is not the product of choice but is caused, and that the causes of crime must be uncovered, particularly those that shape the criminal. In the early twentieth century, in the United States and United Kingdom where it had a particular impact, criminology took a radical new direction, abandoning research into the criminal to turn toward the social context leading to criminality. It thus transformed itself from a biological or psychological discipline into one immersed in sociology. Three schools dominate this period: the group proposing *differential association theory*, the group supporting *social control theory*, and the group positing *strain theory*, all sharing an exclusive concern for social mechanisms. In the 1970s, however, without entirely abandoning its sociological framework, criminology entered a critical new phase. The role of the state, power, and social injustice all entered into the debate, and these changes produced new theories such as *labeling theory*, *critical criminology*, and *feminist criminology*, which no longer looked to undercover the societal conditions leading to criminal behavior, but to question the structure of society itself. During the 1990s, criminology took another new and more concrete direction. Rather than focusing on external, biological, or social causes, new theories—*rational choice*, *routine activity*, and *broken windows* theories—chose to consider criminals as individuals who make choices in the context of specific situations. More recently, criminology has seen a renewed interest in the criminal, whether through the *life-course theory* or by integrating genetic advances into *biosocial* criminology.

Criminology, classical

Classical criminology marks the beginning of criminology, with the first attempt to provide a theory of crime and punishment. It is associated with the Enlightenment, and is based on the general idea that society is founded on a voluntary contract. Establishing a justice system founded on equality and honesty, with legal texts that are written clearly in order to be accessible and understandable, is a necessary condition for establishing consensus around this social contract. In addition, man's actions are thought to be driven by the pursuit of pleasure and the avoidance of pain. The work of Cesare Beccaria (*On Crimes and Punishments*) stemmed from criticism of the penal system then in place, which he saw as arbitrary, barbaric, and ineffective, and fought for the implementation of a new system. Jeremy Bentham saw man as a rational being, who acts in his own interest and who, given the gift of free will, is able to assess gain and loss. Establishing a sentence in fair proportion to the crime should thus act as a deterrent, for if the cost (the sentence) outweighs the gain (the crime), it can be assumed that a reasonable man will not engage in criminal activity. This is not a theory of crime strictly speaking, but rather the development of a penal system able to prevent it.

Criminology, critical

Crime can be approached from the perspective of the individual criminal, as in classical or positivist criminology, through social interactions between individuals, as in social control theory, and through structural dimensions, as in anomie and conflict theory. The so-called "critical criminology" movement, which began in the 1970s, belongs to this latter approach. It is not in fact a theory as such but a generic term covering various theories including neo-Marxism, critical feminism, and abolitionism (see Louk Hulsman), all of which share a view of social structures as constructed by humans and a belief that they can only be changed through demystification. Believing traditional criminology to be futile, at best, these theories consider crime to be a social construct, a transgression of the codes established by institutions, the ruling powers. From their perspective, the true source of criminality is in the structures of domination and the inequalities that result from the conflicts woven into society. These theories therefore generally argue for the expansion of criminal justice into the broader concept of social justice. Furthermore, they do not view crime through its institutional definition, but as social violence or a violation of human rights. They refuse to consider the offender without also considering the society that has led to this situation, criticize the existing order that creates inequalities (whether they are the product of capitalism, the patriarchal order, or racism, etc.), and question the procedures of the justice system, which they see as the exercise of power. Finally, these theories go beyond reform of the justice system to call for an overhaul of society as a whole.

Criminology, cultural

In 1988, Jack Katz published *Seductions of Crime*, a book that introduced a new perspective on criminality by turning attention to the experience of crime, and the feelings and sensations that may accompany it. Taking up this approach, in 1995 Jeff Ferrell and Clinton R. Sanders published their book *Cultural Criminology*.

Cultural criminology takes its departure from *cultural studies*, and inherits its methods, in particular cultural and media analysis. Based on the observation that our world is saturated by media, the circulation of information, and images, and that distinctions between fact and fiction are breaking down, it approaches crime as a collective and in many ways shared experience, that involves symbols, meanings, styles, sensations, and emotions. Unlike conventional criminology, it does not seek to uncover the causes of criminality but rather to analyze the way it is represented and socially constructed, focusing not on hard scientific data but demanding interpretation. Unlike critical criminology, however, it does not regard meaning as produced by social structures, but as resulting from interactions between individuals. In this sense it develops the tradition of qualitative study already present in criminology, which privileges the analysis of individual experiences and the way in which each individual experiences social reality, as opposed to quantitative studies based on statistical data.

Criminology, Marxist

Although Willem Adriaan Bonger provided the first attempt at a Marxist theory of criminology in his 1905 work *Criminality and Economic Conditions*, this early effort failed to gain ground. It was not until the 1970s that serious and concerted efforts were made to develop a Marxist criminology, although even then it was still more a group of kindred spirits than a school, a debate on the approach that should be taken to crime rather than a body of doctrine.

Its early theorists, in particular Richard Quinney, were influenced by the conflict theory that dominated the 1960s. But, like Quinney (*Critique of the Legal Order*, 1974), they reinterpreted this theory from a Marxist perspective, arguing that all the interwoven conflicts structuring the social field are merely the expression of a single conflict, the one between the proletariat and the bourgeoisie. Since it holds the means of production, the bourgeoisie controls the state and manipulates its institutions, such as the justice system, to promote its own interests and perpetuate its power. As a result, all previous theories of criminology are found to be invalid, since whether they were conscious of it or not, the work of traditional, non-Marxist criminologists was produced in the service of the dominant class. This position, accepted in its simplicity by the early theorists, was termed instrumental Marxism (as it considers the law to be an *instrument* in the service of one class) and was modified by its successors (William Chambliss, Jock Young, Ian Taylor, and David Greenberg) who, inspired by Althusser, proposed a structural Marxism. This perspective recognizes that the state has a certain degree of independence, viewing it not in the service of one class but simply as ensuring the social longevity of capitalism, taking multiple interests into account. In parallel, this new version of Marxist criminology reconsidered condemnation of earlier criminological theories, and, as it sought to refine itself, increasingly borrowed from concepts developed by traditional, non-Marxist criminologists, including strain, social control, and social learning theory.

Criminology, positivist

Science was at the forefront in the nineteenth century, and its principles and results were applied in all areas, including society. Where the classical school was based on voluntary actions and free will, the positivist school based its study of criminal behavior on various determinisms. From this perspective, crime is not the result of a choice but is caused or determined by external factors. These factors may be biological, psychological, or social, but may be subject to rigorous scientific study regardless of their nature, since they regulate phenomena in a measurable fashion. In 1876, Cesare Lombroso published the first edition of *Criminal Man*, in which he argued that criminals had a criminal personality, and that the causes of their behavior should therefore be sought in the make-up of their character. Influenced by Darwin's theory of evolution, Lombroso argued that the criminal constitution had an atavistic dimension, a theory that he was pivotal in promoting, along with Raffaele Garofalo and Enrico Ferri. Together they formed the Italian school, which dominated the discipline of criminology from the end of the nineteenth century to the early twentieth century. This school was not fundamentally characterized by its biological approach, but rather by the use of scientific methods, the idea that crime is linked to a pathology, the need for classification, and finally by its concern for the treatment of criminals.

Deterrence

This relates to the use of punishment as a deterrent in order to prevent crime. In the classical theory, crime is considered to be the result of a rational choice that weighs up profit and loss. There is therefore more chance of deterring criminals if the costs involved are high (more difficult to achieve, harsher punishments), particularly if they are certain and immediate.

Punishment inflicted by the law can have a strictly retributive sense, in which criminals pay for the offense they have committed—an approach unconcerned with reducing criminality—or take the form of incarceration, which consists of preventing the offender from committing crimes. It can also, however, be designed as a deterrent. Such punishments are generally divided into two types: general deterrence, which targets potential offenders, and specific deterrence, which targets repeat offenders. Such a view of deterrence is based on a number of hypotheses. It presupposes that man is a rational being who seeks pleasure and avoids suffering, that he is free to choose and to evaluate what is good and bad for him, and finally, that he is aware of the law (for general deterrence) and that he is capable of learning through experience (for specific deterrence). Most proponents of deterrence believe it is most likely to be effective when a) the punishment is certain, b) it is moderately severe, and c) it is swiftly applied.

Differential association theory

The theory of differential association is associated with the work of Edwin Sutherland, and in particularly with his *Principles of Criminology*, which was published in 1939 and revised in 1947. It is within the general framework of his theory, which approaches criminality from a strictly sociological point of view, that Edwin Sutherland sets out the specific concept of differential association. By this he means essentially an interpretation of the law. In his view, one is not born, but rather becomes, a criminal. Criminal behavior primarily results from cultural transmission, and is acquired via first-hand contact with criminal persons or organizations, through which individuals learn not only the techniques but also the reasons, motives, and attitudes that underpin criminal behavior. More precisely, in criminal environments an association forms around a favorable interpretation of transgressing the law. This interpretation is expressed in different ways, and not all criminal environments share the same interpretation (a thief does not necessarily accept murder, for example). It is therefore exposure to this kind of interpretation—which can also originate from non-criminal environments, and which varies according to diverse criteria such as frequency, duration, intensity, or precedent— that favors criminal behavior.

Ecology

The "ecological" approach to the urban phenomenon that characterizes the Chicago School (Robert Ezra Park, Roderick MacKenzie, Ernest Burgess) is a model borrowed from botany and zoology. This envisages plants or animals within, and interacting with, their environment; all individuals, who fight for survival within the environment, are connected to a delicately balanced network of forces. Ecology offers a way to study the interactions and interdependencies that constitute this balance by observing that a group or community may develop different characteristics that give it the appearance of an individual organism, and that several groups can develop symbiotic relationships from which all parties benefit. The view of the city that results from this picture is not as a territory or geographic space, but as a superorganism: a symbiotic unit of individual communities. Botanic ecology also describes a dynamic process of space being occupied as a result of the invasion and then domination of new species that take over the old. Similarly, the dynamics of the city and its areas or neighborhoods are analyzed in terms of invasion, domination, and substitution of both an external (waves of immigration) and internal nature (the development of activity in one neighborhood rather than another). Burgess observes that the city grows not through the automatic addition of elements to its periphery but from its center, in concentric circles that gradually move out further from their point of origin.

Feminist theory

Feminist theories emerged in criminology in the 1960s and 1970s. Although varied and multiple, they had a shared interest in "gender" as a social construct and the recognition of inequalities between "genders." They also criticized classical theories centered on an exclusively male point of view, condemning them in particular for having neglected the role and place of women in their analyses and for unduly generalizing the conclusions they had taken from male criminality to female criminality.

Early feminist research linked to the women's liberation movement, such as Freda Adler's *Sisters in Crime* (1975), argued that as a result of new social conditions, and the growing opportunities for women beyond the domestic sphere, the rate of female crime would also grow. This approach was criticized by other feminist authors for not considering the patriarchal dimension of society, and new avenues were then explored. Liberal feminism, which particularly emphasizes equality, focused on conditions in prisons, the difference between treatment of men and women in the judicial system, and the access of women to different posts within this same judicial system. Socialist feminism concentrated its attention on the traditional family, seen as a space of female oppression, and on the judicial system as another means of oppressing women. Finally, radical feminism, which considers violence to be the ultimate expression of male power over women, particularly highlighted domestic violence, rape, and sexual harassment. More recent feminist theories tend to straddle boundaries, seeking to develop a general theory of criminality that takes into account the dimension of "gender."

Imitation

At the end of the nineteenth century, nascent sociology was forming in France around two major figures: Émile Durkheim and Gabriel Tarde. Their approaches were very different. While Durkheim favored abstract social facts, Tarde's focus was on individual social relationships. In 1890, he published *The Laws of Imitation*, in which he sought to make sense of social reality through individuals, whom he saw not as self-contained but subject to a process of innovation and imitation.

The consistencies that can be observed across society are the result of repetition, or imitation. While for Tarde imitation is an unconscious process, it is nevertheless subject to certain laws: logical laws, which encourage imitation when it is judged that an invention, in line with social trends, is useful in achieving one's goals; and extra-logical laws associated with subjectivity, such as prestige, which mean that it is generally the inferior who imitates the superior. Finally, in Tarde's view, social competition is not economic, but a competition of desires and beliefs, so that strictly speaking it is beliefs and desires that are subject to imitation.

While Tarde did not truly make use of this concept in his approach to crime, it can be found in the theory of differential association developed by Edwin Sutherland, and in the behaviorist approach as taken up by Ronald Akers' social learning theory.

Individual traits

The early twentieth century saw criminology turn away from the positivist school and its biological research toward a sociological approach that it would subsequently retain. During the 1940s and 1950s, however, Sheldon and Eleanor Glueck proposed another model. They argued that while sociological analysis of crime can reveal the conditions that lead to or promote it, they remain general, and such an approach is unable, for example, to explain why individuals subject to the same conditions react differently. Sheldon and Eleanor Glueck thus proposed a multidisciplinary approach to crime that, in addition to environmental conditions, considered biological and personality information, character traits such as impulsivity, irritability, risk propensity, and finally history. This approach would remain largely unpopular. It was not until Hans Jürgen Eysenck's research into personality in England, and the work of Terrie Moffitt on antisocial behavior in the United States, or Jean Pinatel on criminal personality in France, that individual traits and offender histories began to be considered once more. And in John Laub and Robert Sampson's research, with its particular focus on a criminal's history, the Gluecks' theories were truly revived.

Justice

At the root of the changing approach to criminality lies the work of the classical school, and Beccaria. The crux of their interest was not however in criminals or crime, but above all in the workings of justice. These reformers believed it was necessary to abandon an arbitrary approach in order to establish a fair and human justice system. In this sense, crime is seen as an offense, and men are decreed equal before the law, which must not consider either their status or their personality, as an offender is a free man, and the punishment inflicted upon him is nothing more than the retribution due for his offense. With the emergence of positivism, the perspective changed. It became a question of judging the criminal, not the offense. This school also viewed the criminal as a being subject to a variety of biological and social determinants. By emphasizing a scientific rather than legal approach, it proposed to go beyond responsibility in order to consider danger. Here, the role of justice was no longer to punish or re-establish the law that has been transgressed, but to protect society by preventing individuals who presented a risk from causing harm. Experts thus began to appear alongside judges, and sentences were increasingly tailored to individual circumstances. This trend was reinforced by an approach that developed aspects of positivism but discarded its determinism: social defense. In this approach, the primary goal of justice is to protect society, but it is no longer focused solely on the danger posed by the criminal, and also takes rehabilitation into consideration.

These various "philosophies," although in theory mutually exclusive, are in fact jumbled up, with different emphases, in Western legal systems. In France, the law was primarily driven by the classical retribution approach until the emergence of social defense theory in the 1950s, which had a major influence before fading away in the early 1980s. In the United States, in contrast, the idea of rehabilitation was dominant until the 1970s, when its penal system entered a period of crisis. In 1974, Robert Martinson published his famous article "What Works?" (quickly nicknamed "Nothing Works"), in which he expressed skepticism about the effectiveness of rehabilitation, which had no impact on repeat offending in particular, and on the individualization of sentencing, which he saw as a return to discretionary justice. As a result, the United States returned to the classical view of sentencing as retribution or deterrent.

Labeling theory

The criminal act involves not just the criminal, but also society. Arguing that criminology had, until then, considered only one part of the problem by occupying itself exclusively with the criminal, this new approach proposed to complete the picture by focusing on the societal response. From this perspective, crime is seen less as a transgression of norms than as a social interaction between those who are known to have committed a crime and the rest of society.

In his 1938 work *Crime and the Community*, Frank Tannenbaum was the earliest to argue that the first arrest marks a crucial moment in the construction of criminal identity through the "dramatization of evil." In 1951, Edwin Lemert published an article entitled "Primary and Secondary Deviation," in which he distinguished between primary deviation, the transgression of norms, and secondary deviation, the classification, stigmatization, or labeling of this deviance by external authorities. When individuals transgress a norm (primary deviation) their identity is still conventional. It is only when they are stigmatized for this act (secondary deviation) that their identity becomes centered on the fact of deviance. The transgression in itself has no impact on the subject and their status, but rather it is society's reaction to this act, its rejection, that has repercussions and leads to the construction of a deviant identity. External judgments gradually establish the subject in a position of deviance which, if maintained, is finally internalized and leads to the subject embarking on a criminal career. From this point of view it is social control itself that provokes deviance. According to this theory, individuals establish their role as criminals when they are labeled as such; when they are stigmatized, and prevented from taking up conventional roles.

In 1963, Howard Becker provided an expanded version of this theory in *Outsiders*, arguing that deviance is neither a natural, objective reality, nor inscribed in the genes of certain individuals. It is constructed by society, which establishes norms and characterizes the behavior of certain individuals as deviant in regard to these norms.

Life-course theory

The causes of crime can be found in a process of development. The interaction of individual traits with social conditions determines the scale, length, and end of a criminal career. Sociological approaches, which have dominated criminology, took little interest in individual histories, but rather applied their thinking to the social context. In addition, such research focused on the period of adolescence, which is the age with the highest rate of delinquent behavior. During the 1980s and 1990s, particularly following publication of John Laub and Robert Sampson's *Crime in the Making* (1993), some researchers decided to take the periods before and after adolescence into consideration, in order to provide a more complete picture of criminal behavior. This perspective revived the work of Sheldon and Eleanor Glueck. Life-course analysis seeks first and foremost to uncover the reasons for continuity or change occurring between childhood and adulthood, and also seeks to understand the social significance of ages during the course of a life, as well as transmission between generations. It tends to emphasize the role of childhood, rather than simply adolescence, in the path to delinquency, thus highlighting continuity, but also change, and the fact that this process is not preordained but can be stopped ("desistance"). From this perspective, it is not only important to know why someone embarks on a criminal career, and why they continue it, but also why they abandon it.

Madness

Although the medicolegal approach to madness emerged in the seventeenth century, it was during the nineteenth century that it took on its full importance and, particularly in France, established criminology between the two pillars of medicine and the law.

Following the French Revolution, physician Philippe Pinel introduced a new approach to madness. He humanized the treatment of the insane, removing their chains, listening to them, and reorganizing the asylum. He demanded for them to be recognized as patients, not as criminals, and for them to be cared for rather than confined. Finally, in line with this new approach, he proposed a classification of mental illness, which he divided into four groups: melancholia or delirium upon one subject exclusively, mania with or without delirium, dementia, and idiotism. It was the beginning of what was to become psychiatry.

For Pinel, therefore, there was a clear distinction between the madman and the criminal, one which was generally accepted in the early nineteenth century, during which time the justice system sought to apply the law based on Beccaria's classical doctrine. But a series of momentous trials (for crimes including infanticide and cannibalism) upset this certainty. How can an apparently reasonable individual commit monstrous acts? How is it possible to make sense of an apparently motiveless crime? Where is the line between crime and madness? In this context, Pinel's disciple Jean-Étienne Esquirol and his students introduced the idea of "homicidal mania." According to Esquirol, monomania (kleptomania, pyromania, etc.)

resulted from human passion being taken to a degree of pathological excess for which an individual could not be held responsible. "Homicidal mania" was thus presented as a temporary and deadly lack of reason: patients are usually rational beings, but when crises occur they fall under the sway of madness and are no longer responsible for their actions. In the 1820s, this idea found itself at the heart of the battle between the "alienists" (specialists in mental illness) and jurists over application of article 64 of the French Penal Code of 1810, which stated that there could be no crime where the accused was in a state of madness at the time of the action. This battle also affected the medical sphere, for "homicidal mania" posed a problem: it had no etiology other than passion, and since it could be recognized only through the facts—the crime itself—it was very difficult to diagnose.

The middle of the nineteenth century marked a turning point, as the moral approach inherited from Pinel was abandoned, and "homicidal mania" was discarded in favor of apparently more scientific, positivist theories such as Gall's theory of phrenology, Lombroso's theory of atavism, heredity, and Tarde's professional type theory. But it was Bénédict Augustin Morel's theory of degeneration, as developed by Valentin Magnan, that would come to be widely accepted.

Neutralization, techniques of

According to many theories, crime is a matter of learning. Research into subcultures has however primarily focused on the process through which they come to learn, and the actual substance of these subcultures has been little discussed. Generally, they are thought to promote a value system assumed to be an inversion, the reverse of the value system dominant in conventional society. For Graham Sykes and David Matza ("Techniques of Neutralization: A Theory of Delinquency," 1957), however, this is not the case. They observe that when criminals are arrested they feel guilt and shame for their actions and worry about the consequences they will have for their family, even if the family does not support the conventional values of society. Sykes and Matza also reveal criminals' use of a group of justification strategies to excuse their behavior, and propose that criminals do in fact share the values of general society: the criminal subculture does not represent a counterculture, an inversion of these values, but is founded on a number of techniques that tend to neutralize them. They identify various types of denial: of responsibility, of the harm done (which is minimized), and of the victim. Other techniques may also include condemning those who condemn them, or the appeal to a higher loyalty. All of these rationalizations are acquired techniques that enable values to be neutralized and unburdened in the context of criminal activity.

Police

Although the modern police agency was founded in the seventeenth century in France, under Louis XIV, and reconfigured as a "public force" by the revolutionary Constituent Assembly, it was in the United States and United Kingdom from the 1970s onward that a true sociological, rather than purely normative or legal, approach emerged.

The police remains a complex mechanism, with its multiple structures and equally varied functions—maintaining order, managing traffic, controlling crowds, resolving conflicts, obtaining information, and pursuing and arresting offenders—not to mention the many different traditions and national models. It is thus a complex research topic that is difficult to fully grasp. Two broad perspectives in regard to the police can however be distinguished. The first defines the police as having the capacity to use force in a public setting (Egon Bittner), and the second emphasizes its role of maintaining order (James Q. Wilson).

This is the visible face of the police. But there is also an invisible dimension, the "dark" side of the police: its discretionary use of the power it holds. The law applies to all, and the activities of the police are subject to ordinary laws. These laws can however be applied in strict adherence to procedure, or by favoring efficacy over adherence to the rules, and the police as a body has appeared to privilege efficacy above all else and thus to permit itself recourse to illegality in certain circumstances through the use of discretionary power. Research on this topic has revealed a reality of greater complexity, in which illegality is not opposed to the law but leans on it, with a police officer's work thus acting as an authority of the law in an interplay between the police and the public (Donald Black).

Prevention

The post-war period saw an improvement in material living standards and a growth in wellbeing at the same time as an increase in criminality. This cast doubt on the idea that crime was linked to poverty and want, and that social improvements would lead to its decline. In England a new approach emerged, focusing not on the causes of criminal behavior, but envisaging crime as an event. And in 1980, Ronald V. Clarke published his article "Situational Crime Prevention," in which he considered crime rather than criminality, distinguishing between different categories of crime, and the conditions presiding over crime rather than the character of the criminal. These conditions as a whole are no different from those generally presiding over decision-making. Like anyone else, criminals act rationally, seizing opportunities when they present themselves, estimating the costs, and weighing profit against loss. It is therefore possible to consider reducing criminality by reducing opportunities or by making criminal behavior more costly, with the losses outweighing the gains.

Rational choice

The analysis of criminal behavior based on rational choice is a perspective rather than a theory. It began with the observation that criminological theories were trapped in a view of criminal activity as either deviant or pathological, i.e. subject to external social constraints, either impulsive or automatic, and nothing to do with the principles governing ordinary decision-making. This approach, on the other hand, proposes that criminals act rationally, like everyone else, even if the rationality they generally apply is limited.

Rational choice models make use of the economic concept of "cost-benefit analysis": people take rational decisions in so far as they make choices to maximize profits by minimizing losses. This approach borrows from the classical theory of utilitarianism, and is present in classical criminology, but it was not until the 1980s that it emerged in the field of criminology, when the concept of deterrence was revived by Ronald V. Clarke and Derek B. Cornish. It developed through situational crime prevention, which seeks to prevent crime by increasing the obstacles or "costs."

Restorative justice

In 1989 John Braithwaite published *Crime, Shame and Reintegration*, in which he puts his own slant on labeling theories by observing that the shame inflicted on criminals by banishing them from society is in fact a form of stigmatization. The effect of this shame is not only to set criminals apart but also, indirectly, to strengthen criminality by relegating the stigmatized offenders to criminal subcultures. In contrast to some approaches, Braithwaite does not believe that the idea of punishment should be abandoned, but that it should be considered in a different way. Shame is necessary to a community. It enables forgiveness. But for forgiveness to be possible, shame must not stigmatize but enable reintegration; it must enable offenders to return to society and for society to welcome them in return. This approach thus involves a different vision of justice that presents an alternative to the traditional justice system and its twin pillars of retribution and deterrence. This new approach was termed restorative justice. In practice, it involves considering crime primarily as damage to individuals and a community, which must be repaired rather than punished. Reparation is based on a dialogue between all parties involved, as part of a process that aims to heal the harm done to the victim and to the community, leading to a collective decision that will enable reconciliation. The central idea is for offenders to recognize the harm they have done to others and thus experience shame, and consent to repair the damage caused.

Routine activity theory

Unlike other theories, routine activity theory does not focus on the motives behind the criminal act. It seeks to explain the situation of victimization rather than criminal behavior, and concentrates on the environment and events that have enabled the offense to take place.

Environmental aspects—where people live, work, the structural conditions of these different places—and people's lifestyles—where people go, what they do—thus become important elements in analyzing and predicting criminal situations. From this perspective, crime is seen as part of a wider group of routine activities.

In 1972, Oscar Newman published *Defensible Space,* a work in which he argued that urban planning, particularly in cities, was a factor that could favor or indeed deter criminal activity.

In 1979, Marcus Felson and Lawrence Cohen published their article "Social Change and Crime Rate Trends: A Routine Activity Approach," in which they outline their view that crime occurs when a motivated offender, a suitable target, and the absence of a "guardian" are present in a given moment or place. The guardian may be a police officer but is more generally simply a citizen whose presence in the area as a witness suffices to deter an aggressor, and can also be an object such as a light, an anti-theft device, or a security camera. It is the convergence of these three elements that enables a crime to take place. Conversely, changing one of these factors is enough to prevent the crime. The best method of reducing criminality is not therefore to focus on offenders, but to reduce the opportunities for committing crime.

Self-control theory

Social control theories do not generally consider the external mechanisms that enable socialization. But there is another dimension, that of the individual, and the individual's internalization of the process of socialization, which can become a new mechanism in itself. The first theorist to highlight this aspect was Walter Reckless in his article "A New Theory of Delinquency and Crime" (1958), in which he distinguishes between an outer "containment," which broadly corresponds to the concept of traditional social control theory, and his new concept of an inner "containment" (self-image, ability to handle frustration, etc.). In Reckless's view, it is this new dimension that is the critical factor in offending. Developing this analysis and distancing himself from the theory he had outlined in *A Control Theory of Delinquency*, Travis Hirschi, in conjunction with Michael Gottfredson, developed a new approach centered on self-control in *A General Theory of Crime* (1990). A high level of self-control corresponds to a low level of criminal behavior. The four bonds through which an individual is joined to conventional society are thus dependent on the self-control that this individual is able to exert. For Hirschi and Gottfredson, self-control is forged in the earliest moments of socialization, within the family, and is a decisive factor throughout an individual's life. A lack of self-control is associated with the tendency to pursue immediate goals to the detriment of long-term considerations, impulsivity, risk propensity, and unawareness of others: elements that all increase the possibility of an individual engaging in deviant behavior.

Situational crime prevention

In 2002, French law defined this concept as follows:

> Situational crime prevention encompasses the urban planning and architectural measures or techniques designed to prevent offenses from being committed, or to make them less advantageous ...

In 1961, in her classic work *The Death and Life of Great American Cities*, Jane Jacobs drew a link between safety and urban planning.

In 1972, architect and planner Oscar Newman wrote *Defensible Space*, in which he argues that both criminal acts and perceived lack of safety can be reduced through architecture and urban planning.

Criminology professor Ronald V. Clarke complemented this theory with "rational choice" theory, according to which offenders take several factors into account when deciding whether or not to commit a malicious act.

Social bonds

Theories of control can be divided into two perspectives: individual, or social. In the latter case, the criminal act is thought to occur when social bonds are weakened or broken. The stronger the bonds attaching individuals to their parents, adults, and fellow humans, promoting socialization and conformity, the less risk there is that they will break the law.

The standard theory on this topic was outlined by Travis Hirschi in *Causes of Delinquency* (1969), in which he brings together his earlier work and draws out the four elements that constitute the social bond. Firstly, *attachment*: the group of affective relationships that connect us to others and make us concerned for them, their expectations, and their judgment. These others may be parents, teachers, or friends, and in Hirschi's view, it is irrelevant whether those to whom we are attached obey conventional norms, as it is the attachment itself that prevents offending. The second element is *commitment*, which conveys the rational dimension of control. The more committed we are to a conventional activity such as studying, and the more we have invested in terms of time, effort, and money, the more we risk losing through committing a crime. From the perspective of rational choice, the higher cost of such action will prevent us from committing it. The third element is *involvement*. The idea here, almost mechanical, is that involvement in conventional activities such as spending time with family, or being a member of a sports or other type of club, means that there is no leisure time for dreaming of or being engaged in criminal activities. Finally, the fourth element is *belief*. The hypothesis here is not that the offender has a system of beliefs and values different to the dominant system in society, for this would constitute an explanation in itself. Rather, it refers to understanding how and why someone is able to contravene a system of beliefs and values to which he adheres. The response, in this case, is that such adhesion is weakened. Or, inversely, the stronger the adhesion, the lower the risk of offending. As a result, the theory suggests that the weakening of one of these factors, which generally spills over onto the others, increases the risk of offending.

Social control theory

Here, the question posed is: "Why do people not commit crimes?" It seeks to uncover the factors that prevent most people, most of the time, from breaking the law and violating social norms. These theories assume that criminal motivation is widespread; or at least hold a Hobbesian view that left to themselves people would seek to satisfy their interests whatever the cost. If they do not behave in this way, it is because they are surrounded by a system of controls that keeps them within its bounds. The key factor in crime is therefore the absence of control. This approach is situated in the tradition of classical criminology, in which individuals are considered to be rational beings able to calculate and make choices, and, as in the classical theory, it sees people as acting in their own interests above all else. From this perspective man has no natural understanding of moral codes, as they are cultural constructs, and without a social framework he is therefore free to do as he pleases. The existence of this framework enables him to enter into the process of actively choosing to invest in a conventional, non-criminal way of life.

Various theories of control have been developed, the most influential provided by Travis Hirschi in *Causes of Delinquency* (1969). Hirschi describes four types of "social bond" that link adolescents to conventional society: attachment (social and particularly familial links, which indicate sensitivity to the needs and interests of others), commitment (the recognition of the benefits of conventional existence), involvement (the level of involvement in conventional activities during the day), and belief (whether or not feelings concerning what is and what is not acceptable match those of conventional society). Together, these bonds produce the process of socialization. If one or more of these bonds is weakened, control is weakened, and the adolescent is exposed to the temptations of criminal activity.

Social defense theory

Toward the end of the nineteenth century, under pressure from the dispute between alienists and jurists, and with the emergence of positivist criminology, views on criminal law changed. Sentences were no longer viewed as retribution for an act of free will but as a way of protecting society from the danger of criminals. In his 1882 article "Der Zweckgedanke im Strafrecht" (The Idea of Purpose in Criminal Law), also known as the Marburg Program, Franz von Liszt defined sentencing in a civilized state as a goal-oriented voluntary act. A sentence that merely enacts vengeance, on the other hand, has no objective. The social function of sentencing, which depending on the situation consists of helping the offender or protecting society, must therefore be considered. Von Liszt distinguishes between sentences that amend, for offenders who can be helped; sentences that intimidate, for those who do not need to be helped; and sentences that put offenders who cannot be helped in a position where they are unable to do harm. In 1910, Adolphe Prins published "La défense sociale et les transformations du droit penal" (Social Defense and the Transformation of Criminal Law), an article in which, while distancing himself from positivist approaches, he emphasizes the danger posed by offenders, and the need for indeterminate sentences.

In Italy, the concept was taken up post-1945 by Filippo Gramatica, who in *Principi di difesa sociale* (Principles of Social Defense) proposed nothing less than abolishing the system of sentencing, and considering offenders as "antisocial" beings who must first be resocialized outside of the penal system. Gramatica began the "new social defense" movement, which was represented in France by Marc Ancel.

Ancel differed from Gramatica however in arguing, from a humanist and pragmatic perspective, for criminals to be rehabilitated within society. In his view, the goal of criminal law was not to punish or sanction an offense, but to protect society; this protection must be implemented by extralegal means that enable offenders to be kept away or cared for, should emphasize prevention, and seek rehabilitation by foregrounding a human approach to offenders. Ancel further proposed making a distinction between two parts of sentencing: the traditional trial that examines the facts and determines culpability, and the social defense trial, which would examine the offender's personality and determine the punishment. Ancel felt that individuals should be considered to a greater extent than was the case at that time, in particular by drawing upon the resources of the humanities.

Social learning theory

This theory proposes that individuals learn how to behave by modeling themselves on the individuals or groups that they respect. If such models are criminal, there is a strong possibility of them engaging in criminal behavior. Learning is represented by the habits, knowledge, and attitudes resulting from the interplay of reinforcement, gratification, reward, and punishment that individuals experience in their environment.

Gabriel Tarde's 1890 work *The Laws of Imitation* can be regarded as one of the precursors of this approach. Tarde argued that learning—in his view, the origin of criminal behavior—occurs through imitation, reinforced by the proximity of models. In the 1930s and 1940s, Edwin Sutherland proposed his theory of differential association, which suggests that criminal behavior is learned through the interactions that are possible in a criminal environment. In the 1980s, Ronald Akers (*Deviant Behavior: A Social Learning Approach*, 1985) revisited several aspects of psychologist Burrhus F. Skinner's behaviorist theory, and his idea of conditioning, to put forward a more scientific model of Sutherland's theory according to which behavior is determined by the environment and the way it interacts with the individual. Some responses, such as reward, tend to reinforce a type of behavior, while others, such as punishment, tend to discourage it. Individuals exposed to a criminal environment therefore risk being conditioned to adopt criminal behaviors in turn.

Statistics

The classical school sees the criminal act as based on freedom, following which principle we should not expect to observe any regularity in criminal activity. And yet since the first statistical data were produced, in 1827, consistent patterns have in fact emerged, suggesting that crime is also dependent on social factors. Furthermore, penal system reforms, claiming not only a more human but more rational and more effective approach to crime, should have led to a drop in the crime rate, but early statistics actually showed an increase in criminality, particularly in repeat offending. Statistics therefore provide an unexpected but objective view of society and crime that is ripe for interpretation. AndréMichel Guerry's 1833 *Essay on the Moral Statistics of France* represented the first "scientific" criminological approach to statistical data. With the information he had to hand, Guerry sought to prove the idea that criminality was linked to poverty, but finally concluded that it was instead linked to opportunity. Adolphe Quetelet, a Belgian mathematician and astronomer, also observed the patterns of statistical data. Even if the results obtained show merely an average that still allows for the complete freedom of individuals, the patterns they reveal appear to be natural laws ruling social relationships, and thus require a scientific, rather than philosophical or moral, approach to crime.

Although criminology has abandoned its positivist demands in turning toward a sociological approach, it continues to make intensive use of statistics, which not only provide the empirical data on which criminologists develop their theories, but also serve to test their theories by measuring their effects, their ability to explain or prevent criminal phenomena. However, precisely because of their importance, the use of statistical data is not un-problematic. Issues include their reliability—how data are chosen, and the definitions used—their source—do official statistics enable us to interpret crime or simply the activity of the judicial system? Are the statistical investigations carried out in the context of research biased or not biased by the hypotheses of the study?—and finally their interpretation. A great deal of fuel for debate.

Strain theory

The general idea underlying strain theory is that crime is more likely to take place when people are unable to access what they want through legal means. When individuals cannot achieve the goals they seek (money, status, etc.) through the means authorized by society, this creates strain or pressure, and in certain conditions, individuals may respond to strain through crime. These theories aim not only to explain why certain individuals are more likely than others to embark upon a criminal career, but also why the crime rate is higher in certain social groups than in others.

Robert Merton was the first to consider crime in terms of social strain. The approach he put forward in 1938 was that of *anomie,* which later developed into a number of different strain theories. Revisiting Merton's approach in 1955, Albert K. Cohen saw the subculture of the underprivileged youth, particularly that of gangs, as a response to social strain. For Richard Cloward and Lloyd Ohlin, (*Delinquency and Opportunity: A Theory of Delinquent Gangs*, 1960), although social strains predispose to criminal behavior, their nature strongly depends on the environment and the opportunities that it provides. For example, if a gang grows in proximity to a criminal environment willing to train it in the techniques of theft, it tends to commit theft, while if the criminal environment does not provide it with access to illegal means, the gang tends to develop purely violent behavior.

The standard strain theory of the 1950s and 1960s primarily focused on material success. Recent developments aim to expand the field of strains and factors that play a role in choosing a criminal career. Focusing on juvenile delinquency, for example, Robert Agnew 's 1992 work *General Strain Theory* highlights other expectations that can generate strain beyond financial success, such as recognition, autonomy, and status. In addition to the failure to achieve these expectations, he adds two other factors that favor criminal behavior: losing positive stimuli, such as parental divorce or the death of a friend, and exposure to negative stimuli such as insults or aggression.

Subcultural theories

The "subculture", i.e. a group of norms and values within a society to which a particular group is attached, distinct from the dominant norms and values, is a sociological concept. In the context of criminology, it has given rise to a number of different developments.

In his approach to crime, Edwin Sutherland argues that one of the factors conducive to a criminal career is learning the norms, behavior, and views of the criminal world (differential association). Robert Merton and his concept of *anomie* provide a social strain approach. Conflict theory highlights the existence of various "cultures" within the same society, with one of them dominating the others which therefore become subcultures. In 1955, Albert K. Cohen gathered these elements together in his book *Delinquent Boys: The Culture of the Gang*, and put forward the first subcultural theory. In this study, he essentially argues that juvenile delinquency derives from a subculture that rejects the dominant culture and is characterized by the inversion of its values. Unable to meet the expectations of conventional society, a certain group of young people from the underprivileged classes constructs its own system of goals and means by inverting the conventional system, a kind of street culture that can be learned and passed on. In 1958, Walter Miller proposed a slightly different view. Based on an analysis of the underprivileged classes, he suggested that these classes might develop their own subculture whose norms and values were not entirely compatible with those dominant in the rest of the society, thus generating potential conflicts. Criminogenic conditions are to be found in this popular subculture, rather than on the street subculture. In a 1957 article, David Matza and Gresham Sykes looked at the substance supposed to characterize the criminal "subculture," and concluded for their part that the criminal world in fact shares the same norms and values of the rest of society, but merely compartmentalizes its own illegal activity.

Terrorism(s)

Until the attacks organized by Khaled Kelkal in France, terrorism had remained at the fringes of criminology, since it appeared to be politically rather than criminally driven, and was considered to belong to the fields of political science, international relations, or law. Since 1995, the situation has changed substantially. At a time when violent acts are being committed—destructive and murderous, increasingly hybrid, connecting delinquency, criminality, and terror, and affecting society—terrorism has received renewed interest from criminology.

There are however many different definitions of terrorism, and the meaning of the word has itself evolved throughout history, from the Terror of the French Revolution to the Russian nihilists, political organizations such as the Red Army Faction and the PLO, to religiously motivated organizations such as Al-Qaeda. The term also has a dual dimension: in terms of the French Revolution, it designates a method of government, while in terms of the Russian nihilists, it refers to a subversive method of combating the government.

This complexity demonstrates the ever-evolving nature of terrorism. While a number of broad shared traits can be observed—such as the use of violence against civilian populations, the idea of premeditation, and the concept of non-state actors—, in order to provide a complete picture it is necessary to approach the area primarily in terms of its movement and changes, in its plural form, by referring to terrorist "acts" rather than terrorism.

Victimology

It can be said, without prejudice, that crime involves a criminal and his victim. Yet criminology has long focused on the figure of the criminal. Victimology proposes to correct this situation by taking the other side of the equation, the victim, into consideration.

Although the term and idea of "victimology" can be dated to a speech given by Benjamin Mendelsohn in 1947, it was with Hans von Hentig's 1948 article "The Criminal and His Victim" that criminology began to take an interest in the victim of crime, and research began to develop significantly in this area from the 1980s.

There are three main strands of victimology. The first, as represented by Ezzat Fattah, sees victimology as a branch of criminology and focuses on the victims of crime. The second, as represented by John Dussich, broadens the scope of victims to include the victims of accidents or natural disasters. And the third, as represented by Robert Elias, takes a human rights perspective and includes genocide, torture, and slavery.

This still-young discipline is also divided into two approaches which remain to be fully articulated: an academic approach, and an approach more concerned with social action to benefit victims.

Regardless of the approach, victimology tries to understand why and how certain people or groups become victims, and how the crime they have suffered has an impact on their lives.

White-collar crime

This expression was introduced by Edwin Sutherland in his 1949 book *White Collar Crime*, in which he defined it as "a crime committed by a person of respectability and high social status in the course of his occupation." This definition is notable in not specifying the nature of the offense or its motivations, but focusing on the status and conditions of the crime. For Sutherland, it was primarily important to draw attention to a sector of criminality that he felt had been neglected by other researchers of the period, who focused on the underprivileged classes, in which crime rates were highest. For Sutherland, white-collar crime was no different from ordinary crime and was learned in the same way, following the same process of differential association. The world of business is permeated with criminal attitudes and behaviors, which are adopted by new entrants who learn to rationalize their actions, and pass them on to their successors. Furthermore, since crime is primarily associated with the underprivileged classes, business practices are technical and difficult to decode, and finally because free enterprise resists regulation, the world of business finds itself in a blind spot in which the behavior of its members is rarely exposed to condemnation. This produces a particular form of anomie that favors deviance.

Part Two

KEY WORKS

a

Adler, Freda
Sisters in Crime[1]

Women are no longer indentured to the kitchens, baby
carriages or bedrooms of America. The skein of myths
about women is unraveling, the chains have been pried
loose, and there will be no turning back to the days when
women found it necessary to justify their existence by
producing babies or cleaning houses. Allowed their
freedom for the first time, women—by the tens of thousands—have chosen to desert those kitchens and plunge
exuberantly into the formerly all-male quarters of the
working world.

[...]

In the same way that women are demanding equal opportunity in fields of legitimate endeavour, a similar
number of determined women are forcing their way into
the world of major crimes.

[...]

It is this segment of women who are pushing into—and
succeeding at—crimes which were formerly committed
by males only. Females like Marge are now being found
not only robbing banks single-handedly, but also committing assorted armed robberies, muggings, loan-shark-
ing operations, extortion, murders, and a wide variety of

---

1   *Sisters in Crime: The Rise of the New Female Criminal* (New York:
    McGraw Hill, 1975).

other aggressive, violence-oriented crimes which previously involved only men.

[...]

By every indicator available, female criminals appear to be surpassing males in the rate of increase for almost every major crime. Although males continue to commit the greater number of offences, it is the women who are committing those same crimes at yearly rates of increase now running as high as six or seven times faster than males.

[...]

In summary, what we have described is a gradual but accelerating social revolution in which women are closing many of the gaps, social and criminal, that have separated them from men. The closer they get, the more alike they look and act. This is not to suggest that there are no inherent differences. Differences do exist and will be elaborated later in this book but it seems clear that those differences are not of prime importance in understanding female criminality. The simplest and most accurate way to grasp the essence of women's changing patterns is to discard dated notions of femininity. This is a role that fewer and fewer women are willing to play. In the final analysis, women criminals are human beings who have basic needs and abilities and opportunities. Over the years these needs have not changed, nor will they. But women's abilities and opportunities have multiplied, resulting in a kaleidoscope of changing patterns whose final configuration will be fateful for all of us.

Akers, Roland L.

Deviant Behavior: A Social Learning Approach [2]

This theory integrates Edwin H. Sutherland's *differential association theory* of violations of social and legal norms with principles of modern learning theory. Sutherland's theory as he finally stated in 1947 is in the form of [...] nine declarative statements (Sutherland and Cressey, 1970, 75-77).

Although the entire set of statements collectively make up the theory of differential association, the sixth statement was referred to by Sutherland as the "principle of differential association" and is seen as the heart of the theory; it is that *one commits criminal acts because his accepted "definitions" of law as something to violate are in "excess" of his accepted definitions of the law as something that can, must, or should be obeyed.* Thus, it is not a simple theory of associating with "bad companions"; rather, it is concerned with contact with criminal patterns and definitions (normative evaluations) *balanced against* contact with conforming definitions, whether this contact comes from association with those who commit crime or with those who are law-abiding (Cressey, 1960, 49).

[...]

1. Deviant behavior is learned according to the principles of operant conditioning.

2. Deviant behavior is learned both in nonsocial situations that are reinforcing or discriminating

---

2   *Deviant Behavior: A Social Learning Approach* (Belmont: Wadsworth, 3rd edition, 1985).

and through that social interaction in which the behavior of other persons is reinforcing or discriminating for such behavior.

3. The principal part of the learning of deviant behavior occurs in those groups which comprise or control the individual's major source of reinforcements.

4. The learning of deviant behavior, including specific techniques, attitudes, and avoidance procedures, is a function of the effective and available reinforcers and the existing reinforcement contingencies.

5. The specific class of behavior learned and its frequency of occurrence are a function of the effective and available reinforcers, and the deviant or non-deviant direction of the norms, rules, and definitions which in the past have accompanied the reinforcement.

6. The probability that a person will commit deviant behavior is increased in the presence of normative statements, definitions, and verbalizations which, in the process of differential reinforcement of such behavior over conforming behavior, have acquired discriminative value.

7. The strength of deviant behavior is a direct function of the amount, frequency, and probability of its reinforcement. The modalities of association with deviant patterns are important insofar as they affect the source, amount, and scheduling of reinforcement.

These seven statements contain terms which need definition and present only an outline of the theory; reference to only these seven statements will not give the full substance of the theory. The remaining discussion in this chapter is to define and clarify terms; explain the theory more fully; present the way it has been developed, criticized, and tested, and show how it will be applied ...

b

Beccaria, Cesare
On Crimes and Punishments[3]

Let us open our history books, and we shall see that laws, which are or ought to be agreements among free men, usually have been the instrument of the passions of a few persons. Sometimes laws arise from a fortuitous and transient necessity, but they have never been dictated by an impartial observer of human nature who can grasp the actions of a multitude of men and consider them from this point of view: *the greatest happiness shared among the greatest number*. Happy are those very few nations that have not waited for the slow movement of happenstance and human vicissitudes to make excessive evil give way to progress toward goodness but that have accelerated the intermediate stages with good laws! Further, mankind owes a debt of gratitude to the philosopher who, from the despised obscurity of his study, had the courage to cast the first and long fruitless seeds of useful truths among the multitude!

We now know the proper relationships between subject and sovereign and among different nations; commerce has been quickened by the appearance of philosophic truths spread by the printing press, and a quiet war of industry has broken out among nations, the most humane sort of war and the kind most worthy of reasonable men.

---

3   Introduction to On Crimes and Punishments [1764], trans. David Young (Indianapolis: Hackett Publishing Company, 1986).

These are the fruits that we owe to the enlightenment of this century. Very few people, however, have examined and fought against the cruelty of punishments and the irregularity of criminal procedure, a part of legislation that is so fundamental and so neglected almost everywhere in Europe. Very few people, by going back to general principles, have destroyed the errors accumulated over several centuries, or at least used the strength of recognized truth to check the unbridled course of ill-directed power, which, up to now, has set a long and supposedly authoritative example of cold-blooded atrocity. And yet the trembling of the weak, sacrificed to cruel ignorance and wealthy indolence; the barbarous and useless tortures multiplied with prodigal and useless severity for crimes that are either unproven or chimerical; the squalor and horrors of a prison, augmented by uncertainty, that most cruel tormentor of the wretched—these should have aroused the attention of the kind of magistrates who guide the opinions of human minds.

The immortal President de Montesquieu touched hastily on this matter. Indivisible truth has compelled me to follow the shining footsteps of this great man. The thinking men for whom I write, however, will know how to tell my trail from his. I shall count myself fortunate if I, as did he, can earn the secret gratitude of the little-known and peace-loving followers of reason and if I can inspire that sweet thrill with which sensitive souls respond to whoever upholds the interests of humanity!

Becker, Howard
Outsiders[4]

The sociological view [...] defines deviance as the infraction of some agreed-upon rule. It then goes on to ask who breaks rules, and to search for the factors in their personalities and life situations that might account for the infractions.

[...]

Such an assumption seems to me to ignore the central fact about deviance: it is created by society. I do not mean this in the way it is ordinarily understood, in which the causes of deviance are located in the social situation of the deviant or in "social factors" which prompt this action. I mean, rather, that *social groups create deviance by making the rules whose infraction constitutes deviance,* and by applying those rules to particular people and labeling them as outsiders. From this point of view, deviance is *not* a quality of the act the person commits, but rather a consequence of the application by others of rules and sanctions to an "offender." The deviant is one to whom that label has successfully been applied; deviant behavior is behavior that people so label.

---

4   *Outsiders: Studies in the Sociology of Deviance* (New York: The Free Press, 1963).

Bentham, Jeremy
Treatise on Civil and Penal Legislation[5]

The public good ought to be the object of the legislator; *general utility* ought to be the foundation of his reasonings. To know the true good of the community is what constitutes the science of legislation; the art consists in finding the means to realize that good.

The principle of *utility*, vaguely announced, is seldom contradicted; it is even looked upon as a sort of commonplace in politics and morals. But this almost universal assent is only apparent. The same ideas are not attached to this principle; the same value is not given to it; no uniform and logical manner of reasoning results from it.

To give it all the efficacy which it ought to have, that is, to make it the foundation of a system of reasonings, three conditions are necessary.

First,—to attach clear and precise ideas to the word *utility*, exactly the same with all who employ it.

Second,—to establish the unity and the sovereignty of this principle, by rigorously excluding every other. It is nothing to subscribe to it in general; it must be admitted without any exception.

Third,—to find the processes of a moral arithmetic by which uniform results may be arrived at.

---

5   "The Principle of Utility," in *Theory of Legislation*, Vol. 1, trans. from the French of Etienne Dumont by R. Hildreth (Boston: Weeks, Jordan, & Company, 1802).

The causes of dissent from the doctrine of utility may all be referred to two false principles, which exercise an influence, sometimes open and sometimes secret, upon the judgments of men. If these can be pointed out and excluded, the true principle will remain in purity and strength.

These three principles are like three roads which often cross each other, but of which only one leads to the wished-for destination. The traveller turns often from one into another, and loses in these wanderings more than half his time and strength. The true route is however the easiest; it has mile-stones which cannot be shifted, it has inscriptions, in a universal language, which cannot be effaced; while the two false routes have only contradictory directions in enigmatical characters. But without abusing the language of allegory, let us seek to give a clear idea of the true principle, and of its two adversaries.

Nature has placed man under the empire of *pleasure* and *pain*. We owe to them all our ideas; we refer to them all our judgments, and all the determinations of our life. He who pretends to withdraw himself from this subjection, knows not what he says. His only object is to seek pleasure and to shun pain, even at the very instant that he rejects the greatest pleasures or embraces pains the most acute. These eternal and irresistible sentiments ought to be the great study of the moralist and the legislator. The *principle of utility* subjects every thing to these two motives.

Utility is an abstract term. It expresses the property or tendency of a thing to prevent some evil or to procure some good. *Evil* is pain, or the cause of pain. *Good* is pleasure, or the cause of pleasure. That which is conformable to the utility, or the interest of an individual, is what tends to augment the total sum of his happiness. That which is conformable to the utility, or the interest of a community, is what tends to augment the total sum of the happiness of the individuals that compose it.

A *principle* is a first idea, which is made the beginning or basis of a system of reasonings. To illustrate it by a sensible image, it is a fixed point to which the first link of a chain is attached. Such a principle must be clearly evident;—to illustrate and to explain it, must secure its acknowledgement. Such are the axioms of mathematics; they are not proved directly; it is enough to show that they cannot be rejected without falling into absurdity.

The *logic of utility* consists in setting out, in all the operations of the judgment, from the calculation or comparison of pains and pleasures, and in not allowing the interference of any other idea.

I am a partisan of the *principle of utility* when I measure my approbation or disapprobation of a public or private act by its tendency to produce pleasure or pain; when I employ the words *just, unjust, moral, immoral, good, bad,* simply as collective terms including the ideas of certain pains or pleasures; it being always understood that I use the words *pain* and *pleasure* in their ordinary signification, without inventing any arbitrary definition for the sake of excluding certain pleasures or denying the existence of certain pains. In this matter we want no refinement, no metaphysics. It is not necessary to consult Plato, nor Aristotle. *Pain* and *pleasure* are what every body feels to be such—the peasant and the prince, the unlearned as well as the philosopher.

He who adopts the *principle of utility*, esteems virtue to be a good only on account of the pleasures which result from it; he regards vice as an evil only because of the pains which it produces. Moral good is *good* only by its tendency to produce physical good. Moral evil is *evil* only by its tendency to produce physical evil; but when I say *physical*, I mean the pains and pleasures of the soul as well as the pains and pleasures of sense. I have in view man, such as he is, in his actual constitution.

If the partisan of the *principle of utility* finds in the common list of virtues an action from which there results more pain than pleasure, he does not hesitate to regard that pretended virtue as a vice; he will not suffer himself to be imposed upon by the general error; he will not lightly believe in the policy of employing false virtues to maintain the true.

If he finds in the common list of offences some indifferent action, some innocent pleasure, he will not hesitate to transport this pretended offence into the class of lawful actions; he will pity the pretended criminals, and will reserve his indignation for their persecutors.

Bertillon, Alphonse
On Identification by Anthropometric Measurements [6]

[...]

When an individual who has already been convicted on one or several occasions is arrested for another crime or offense, it is greatly in his interest to conceal his true name, and to evade questions about his past. He knows that his as-yet uncertain conviction will become well-nigh inevitable if his criminal past becomes known.

With his anonymity he obstructs all enquiries, prevents discovery of his accomplices, the location of the stolen goods, etc. ... and also avoids the heavier sentence he might receive as a repeat offender.

[...]

Around ten to twelve years ago, it seemed that photography would be of great assistance in the identification of repeat offenders. The police photographed all convicted criminals. But this method soon became impractical.

[...]

Until now the police and the justice system behind it have been caught in a vicious circle, taking photographs in order to retrieve a repeat offender's name, but requiring a name to find a photograph taken on a previous occasion.

---

6   "De l'identification par les signalements anthropométriques." Lecture delivered to the International Penal and Prison Congress in Rome, November 22, 1885, published in *Archives de l'Anthropologie Criminelle et des Sciences Pénales* 1 (1886): 193-221.

The method I outline enables the previously measured photograph of a repeat offender to be retrieved by its numbered measurements alone.

The photographs are first divided by sex: men on one side, and women on the other.

The remaining men can then be divided into three groups based on height, namely individuals:

- Of small and very small height

- Of average height

- Of large and very large height

Each of these three core groups should then be divided again, based on the same principle, and, with no further reference to height, into three groups according to the length of each individual's head. These nine new subdivisions will then contain:

- small and very small heads; average heads; large and very large heads.

These subdivisions are then divided into three groups according to foot length, thus comprising:

- Small and very small feet; average feet; large and very large feet.

Arm span provides a fourth indication for dividing each of the previous packets of photographs into another three groups, which can be divided again into smaller elements, based on the individual's approximate age, eye color,[7] and middle finger length.

The prefecture's collection of photographs can thus be divided into groups of around fifty photographs, which are then much easier to browse.

---

7   Alphonse Bertillon developed a novel way to describe eye color, a method he applied to over 25,000 sets of anthropometric measurements over two years. Bertillon divided eye color into seven classes: eyes with a yellow tint; orange tint; chestnut-brown tint; brown tint grouped around the pupil; brown tint with a number of greenish striations; and pure brown. See Alphonse Bertillon, "La couleur de l'iris, exposé à la nomenclature des nuances de l'oeil telle qu'elle est adoptée par le service d'identification au dépôt de la Préfecture de police de Paris et dans le service pénitentiaire de France", *Annales de la Démographie Internationale,* Vol. 7 (1883), 226-246.

Bittner, Egon
The Functions of the Police in Modern Society[8] *(1970)*

It is, of course, not surprising that a society committed to the establishment of peace by pacific means and to the abolishment of all forms of violence from the fabric of its social relations, at least as a matter of official morality and policy, would establish a corps of specially deputized officials endowed with the exclusive monopoly of using force contingently where limitations of foresight fail to provide alternatives. That is,given the melancholy appreciation of the fact that the total abolition of force is not attainable, the closest approximation to the ideal is to limit it as a special and exclusive trust. If it is the case, however, that the mandate of the police is organized around their capacity and authority to use force, i.e., if this is what the institution's existence makes available to society, then the evaluation of that institution's performance must focus on it. While it is quite true that policemen will have to be judged on other dimensions of competence, too—for example, the exercise of force against criminal suspects requires some knowledge about crime and criminal law—their methods as society's agents of coercion will have to be considered central to the overall judgment.

The proposed definition of the police role entails a difficult moral problem. How can we arrive at a favorable or even accepting judgment about an activity which is, in its very conception, opposed to the ethos of the polity

---

8   *The Functions of the Police in Modern Society: A Review of Background Factors, Current Practices, and Possible Role Models* (Chevy Chase, MD: National Institute of Mental Health, Center for Studies of Crime and Delinquency, 1970).

that authorizes it? Is it not well nigh inevitable that this mandate be concealed in circumlocution? While solving puzzles of moral philosophy is beyond the scope of this analysis, we will have to address this question in a somewhat more mundane formulation: namely, on what terms can a society dedicated to peace institutionalize the exercise of force?

It appears that in our society two answers to this question are acceptable. One defines the targets of legitimate force as enemies and the coercive advance against them as warfare. Those who wage this war are expected to be possessed by the military virtues of valor, obedience and *esprit de corps*. The enterprise as a whole is justified as a sacrificial and glorious mission in which the warrior's duty is "not to reason why." The other answer involves an altogether different imagery. The targets of force are conceived as practical objectives and their attainment a matter of practical expediency. The process involves prudence, economy, and considered judgment, from case to case. The enterprise as a whole is conceived as a public trust, the exercise of which is vested in individual practitioners who are personally responsible for their decisions and actions.

Reflection suggests that the two patterns are profoundly incompatible. Remarkably, however, our police departments have not been deterred from attempting the reconciliation of the irreconcilable. Thus, our policemen are exposed to the demand of a conflicting nature in that their actions are supposed to reflect military prowess and professional acumen.

Black, Donald
The Manners and Customs of the Police[9] *(1980)*

Most arrest situations arise through citizen rather than police initiative. In this sense, the criminal process is invoked in a manner not unlike that of private-law systems that are mobilized through a reactive process, depending upon the enterprise of citizen claimants in pursuit of their own interests (see Chapter 2 of the present volume). In criminal law as in other areas of public law, although the state has the formal authority to bring legal actions on its own initiative, the average case is the product of a citizen complaint.

One implication of this pattern is that most criminal cases pass through a moral filter in the citizen population before the state assumes its enforcement role. A major portion of the responsibility for criminal-law enforcement is thus kept out of police hands. Much like courts in the realm of private law, then, the police operate as moral servants of the citizenry. A further implication of this pattern is that the deterrence function of the criminal process to an important degree depends upon citizen willingness to mobilize the criminal law, just as the deterrence function of private law depends so much upon citizen plaintiffs. Sanctions cannot deter illegal behavior if the law lies dormant because of an inefficient mobilization process. In this sense, all legal systems rely to a great extent upon private citizens.

---

9   *The Manners and Customs of the Police* (New York, London: Academic Press, 1980).

Bottoms, Anthony
*"Theoretical Reflections on the Evaluation
of a Penal Policy Initiative"*[10]

What is crucial in understanding legally compliant behavior, however, is not merely to formulate a reason-
ably precise taxonomy of the principal mechanisms of
compliance, but also to specify how these mechanisms
might interact with one another. For example, successful
situational crime prevention of the "target hardening"
variety has its immediate impact by (perforce) strength-
ening constraint-based compliance; but, as news of the
strengthened defence of the relevant target spreads
among potential offenders, there may well also be a deterrent (instrumental) effect.

The principal contribution of the IEP (Incentives and
Earned Privileges) research, in this context, is to illustrate a particular kind of interaction between instrumental and normative mechanisms. One example of
instrumental-normative interaction is well known to
those versed in the literature on deterrence: in summary, it is that *deterrence works best among these with strong
normative bonds to law-abiding members of the community*
(sometimes expressed as "stakes in conformity"). The
present study differs from that example in two ways: first,
as regards instrumental mechanisms, it focuses on incentives rather than disincentives; and secondly, as regards
normative mechanisms, it focuses on legitimacy rather
than attachment. We can formulate the interaction ef-

---

10   "Theoretical Reflections on the Evaluation of a Penal Policy
Initiative," in *The Criminal Foundations of Penal Policy: Essays in
Honour of Roger Hood,* eds. Lucia Zedner and Andrew Ashworth
(Oxford: Oxford University Press, 2003), 107-194.

fect that is illustrated by the IEP research in something like the following language: *incentive-based policies may be partially or wholly undermined in their intended effects if they are administered in what the subjects of the policy regard as an unfair way, and especially if these perceptions can be shown to be justified in terms of widely-shared moral beliefs in the society in question.*

[...]

Thus, *incentives policies in criminal justice can be successful,* but those who formulate them must always remember that legal compliance is multifaceted, and that an incentives policy, as operationalized, may well have interactive links with other potential mechanisms of compliance or non-compliance, notably those of fairness and legitimacy. If unfairness in operation (for example arbitrary and inconsistent decision-making) can be avoided, then there is no reason to suppose that an incentives policy will fail.

[...]

From a strictly rational-choice perspective arbitrariness and inconsistency constitute inefficiency; but to those who are subjected to them, they are also often seen as unfair. Thus, certain kinds of *inefficiencies in a rational-choice approach can themselves generate normative disengagement,* and perhaps even help to trigger a wider delegitimation of the authority.

Braithwaite, John
Crime, Shame and Reintegration[11]

The theory in this book suggests that the key to crime control is cultural commitments to shaming in ways that I call reintegrative. Societies with low crime rates are those that shame potently and judiciously; individuals who resort to crime are those insulated from shame over their wrongdoing. However, shame can be applied injudiciously and counterproductively; the theory seeks to specify the types of shaming which cause rather than prevent crime.

[...]

The first step to productive theorizing about crime is to think about the contention that labeling offenders makes things worse. The contention is both right and wrong. The theory of reintegrative shaming is an attempt to specify when it is right and when wrong. The distinction is between shaming that leads to stigmatization—to outcasting, to confirmation of a deviant master status—versus shaming that is reintegrative, that shames while maintaining bonds of respect or love, that sharply terminates disapproval with forgiveness, instead of amplifying deviance by progressively casting the deviant out. Reintegrative shaming controls crime; stigmatization pushes offenders toward criminal subcultures.

[...]

The theory of reintegrative shaming posits that the consequence of stigmatization is attraction to criminal sub-

---

11   *Crime, Shame and Reintegration* (Cambridge: Cambridge University Press, 1989).

cultures. Subcultures supply the outcast offender with the opportunity to reject her rejectors, thereby maintaining a form of self-respect. In contrast, the consequence of reintegrative shaming is that criminal subcultures appear less attractive to the offender. Shaming is the most potent weapon of social control unless it shades into stigmatization. Formal criminal punishment is an ineffective weapon of social control partly because it is a degradation ceremony with maximum prospects for stigmatization.

The nub of the theory of reintegrative shaming is therefore about the effectiveness of reintegrative shaming and the counterproductivity of stigmatization in controlling crime. In addition, the theory posits a number of conditions that make for effective shaming. Individuals are more susceptible to shaming when they are enmeshed in multiple relationships of interdependency; societies shame more effectively when they are communitarian. Variables like urbanization and residential mobility predict communitarianism, while variables like age and gender predict individual interdependency [...].

Some of the ways that the theory of reintegrative shaming builds on earlier theories should now be clear. Interdependency is the stuff of control theory; stigmatization comes from labeling theory; subculture formation is accounted for in opportunity theory terms; subcultural influences are naturally in the realm of subcultural theory; and the whole theory can be understood in integrative cognitive social learning theory terms such as are provided by differential association.

Brodeur, Jean-Paul
"The Police: Myths and Realities"[12]

Two positions have remained relatively unchanged since the beginning of empirical research on the police, which can be dated to William Westley's work on the police department in Gary, Indiana, around 1950.

The first of these positions establishes a constitutive relationship between police work and the concepts of violence and coercion. The particular nature of the relationship between the police and its citizens is its symmetry, or rather its reciprocity: the police officers studied by Westley and later by Ker Muir and various others *perceive* the situations in which they intervene under the cloud of a threat to their own safety. In a reciprocal fashion, an entire tradition of American sociology, most actively represented by Egon Bittner, sees recourse to coercive force as the defining characteristic of policing. In France, Loubet del Bayle, working in the Weberian tradition, also sees the police as the coercive appendage of the state, and this idea has received support from radical criminologists who have discussed policing in collections edited by Platt and Cooper and by the Center for Research on Criminal Justice.

The second position that can be observed is the sustained denial that the *essential* (or principal) role of the police, whether in theory or practice, is to crack down on crime. The mandate of the police is seen instead to reside in maintaining public order, a concept that has regrettably expanded in a rather vague manner. One of the earliest

---

12 "La police: mythes et réalités," *Criminologie* 17, no. 1 (1984): 9-41.

and most energetic supporters of this idea was James Q. Wilson, and it has now been taken up enthusiastically by Peter Manning (see Manning and Van Maanen), one of the most influential American researchers, and by British theorists such as Evans and Alderson. Empirical analysis of the actual use of police working time repeatedly confirms Wilson's theory.

Brodeur, Jean-Paul
"Marxist Criminology: Recent Controversies"[13]

Among the humanities, criminology is one of the disciplines in which Marxist theory has had the most belated impact (early attempts from Bonger and from Rusche and Kirchheimer did not gain traction). It is therefore possible to predict its future evolution based on recent developments in the other social sciences, and thus anticipate a gradual decline in the influence of dialectical materialism and historical materialism. Such a waning is in fact already apparent.

I believe it is necessary to avoid two pitfalls in establishing a criminological approach based on Marxist theory. First, it would be consciously impoverishing to strike out the materialist episode from criminology and regress to approaches that have been decisively discarded by Marxist criticism. There is at least one aspect of Marx's thought that can be legitimately termed unsurpassable: the requirement to submit the field as a whole to the ideal of a test hypothesizing its production by particular historically located interests. This demystifying hypothesis, it must be emphasized, will never in itself suffice; but the evaluation of its validity does constitute an irreplaceable test for judging what is presented as unconditionally just, good or true. This first theoretical test leads to coherent and rigorous practice.

The second pitfall lies in the prescriptions of a voluntaristic eschatology, according to which we must consent to close our eyes to the inadequacies of materialism in

---

13   "La criminologie marxiste: controverses récentes," *Déviance et Société* 8, no. 1 (1984): 43-70.

order to avoid feeding reaction, and persist on building a school of criminology on a theoretical foundation that is cracking and crumbling away. And yet it is precisely this anxious eschatology, according to which an imaginary socialism—whose historical embodiment appears increasingly oppressive—would constitute the panacea for all the evils of criminal justice, that generates and feeds the reaction, if only by the irritated weariness that it provokes. Most importantly, the object of this voluntarism—the production of a doctrinarian and militant materialist criminology—is increasingly hollow: one of the persuasive findings in the overview I have presented is the very apparent erosion of the Marxist paradigm in both its theoretical foundation, which is increasingly marked by syncretism, and in its practice, which is rediscovering the decried values of reformism. While there is reason to rejoice in some of radical criminology's rediscoveries—such as the brutal reality of victimization, for example—it is also important to highlight the difficulties associated with repurposing. One of the difficulties most at fault is the fall of repurposed discourse into sectarian banalities and ultimately solipsism: the reinvention of the wheel interests only those who have added their spokes.

Finally, there is an important homology between Marxist criminology and traditional criminology, which I have not yet discussed, reserving my remarks for the conclusion of this book. We can distinguish between two forms of universalism. The first form, which I will call essential, is expressed in the affirmation of the ahistoric permanence of certain phenomena, and for the most part leads to the endless trotting out of platitudes such as: "There always has been crime and there always will be," "humanity is characterized by a natural sense of justice," "the social order has always been maintained by the enactment of good laws," etc. The second form of universalism, which often goes unperceived, is of a formal and methodological nature: although the fundamentally historical nature of the objects of knowledge is explicitly recognized, this recognition is accompanied by a rigid assumption of the uniqueness of the procedure that is to produce knowledge of these objects. Phenomena are declared to be varying, multiple, and transitory, but the method of observing them is itself determined, its end supposedly lying in the constitution of an assimilating and all-encompassing body of knowledge. While materialism in part developed by making inroads into the epistemological field of some of the most cumbersome universal essentials, it has never renounced formal universalism and its demand for the assimilation of knowledge is of exemplary rigor, comparable to that of positivism and other specific variants of traditional criminology.

I believe that formal universalism is, for some practical theorists, as problematic as posing essential universals. The field of criminology is constituted by phenomena that are often heterogeneous, their shared features artificially conferred by the vicissitudes of social reaction. In my view, the discipline thus forms the ultimate example of those theoretical practices whose assimilating nature ought to be challenged.

Burgess, Ernest W.
"The Study of the Delinquent as a Person"[14]

Sociology is now undergoing a transformation like that which has almost completely changed psychology from metaphysics to an experimental science. From a philosophy of society sociology is emerging into a science of society. Consequently the interest of the new sociology is now turned to defining the experimental point of view, to classifying problems for investigation, and to developing a technique of research.

Not only criminality, but all social problems, indeed the entire area of group behaviour and social life, is being subjected to sociological description and analysis. The person is conceived in his interrelations with the social organization, with the family, the neighbourhood, the community, and society. Explanations of his behaviour are found in terms of human wishes and social attitudes, mobility and unrest, intimacy and status, social contacts and social interaction, conflict, accommodation and assimilation.

The study of a delinquent as a person opens up a fertile field. Materials in the form of case-records, personal documents, and life-histories, are now available for analysis. Psychiatry and psychology in attacking the problem of the criminal from the standpoint of individual behaviour have made contributions of high value, which have prepared the way for sociological research. The psychiatric, psychological, and sociological methods of investigation are not in conflict with each other but rather comple-

---

14 "The Study of the Delinquent as a Person," *American Journal of Sociology* 28, no. 6 (May 1923): 657-680.

mentary and interdependent. The sociologist will continue to rely upon the findings of these other sciences of behaviour for a knowledge of individual differences in mentality and temperament, while they in turn will be disposed to look to sociology for light upon the adjustment of the person in the social organization.

C

Cloward, Richard A.
Ohlin, Lloyd
Delinquency and Opportunity:
A Theory of Delinquent Gangs[15]

The concept of differential opportunity structures permits us to unite the theory of anomie, which recognizes the concept of differentials in access to legitimate means, and the "Chicago tradition," in which the concept of differentials in access to illegitimate means is implicit. We can now look at the individual, not simply in relation to one or the other system of means, but in relation to both legitimate and illegitimate systems. This approach permits us to ask, for example, how the relative availability of illegitimate opportunities affects the resolution of adjustment problems leading to deviant behavior. We believe that the way in which these problems are resolved may depend upon the kind of support for one or another type of illegitimate activity that is given at different points in the social structure. If, in a given social location, illegal or criminal means are not readily available, then we should not expect a criminal subculture to develop among adolescents. By the same logic, we should expect the manipulation of violence to become a primary avenue to higher status only in areas where the means of violence are not denied to the young. To give a third example, drug addiction and participation in subcultures organized around the consumption of drugs presuppose

---

15 *Delinquency and Opportunity: A Theory of Delinquent Gangs* (Glencoe: The Free Press, 1960).

that persons can secure access to drugs and knowledge about how to use them. In some parts of the social structure, this would be very difficult; in others, very easy. In short, there are marked differences from one part of the social structure to another in the types of illegitimate adaptation that are available to persons in search of solutions to problems of adjustment arising from the restricted availability of legitimate means. In this sense, then, we can think of individuals as being located in two opportunity structures—one legitimate, the other illegitimate. Given limited access to success-goals by legitimate means, the nature of the delinquent response that may result will vary according to the availability of various illegitimate means.

Cohen, Albert K.
Delinquent Boys: The Culture of the Gang[16]

What we see when we look at the delinquent subculture (and we must not even assume that this describes *all juvenile crime*) is that it is *non-utilitarian, malicious,* and *negativistic.* We usually assume that when people steal things, they steal because they want them. They may want them because they can eat them, wear them or otherwise use them; or because they can sell them; or even—if we are given to a psychoanalytic turn of mind—because on some deep symbolic level they substitute or stand for something unconsciously desired but forbidden. All of these explanations have this in common, that they assume that the stealing is a means to an end, namely, the possession of some object of value, and that it is, in this sense, rational and "utilitarian." However, the fact cannot be blinked—and this fact is of crucial importance in defining our problem—that much gang stealing has no such motivation at all. Even where the value of the object stolen is itself a motivating consideration, the stolen sweets are often sweeter than those acquired by more legitimate and prosaic means. In homelier language, stealing "for the hell of it" and apart from considerations of gain and profit is a valued activity to which attaches glory, prowess, and profound satisfaction. There is no accounting in rational and utilitarian terms for the effort expended and the danger run in stealing things which are often discarded, destroyed, or casually given away. A group of boys enters a store where each takes a hat, a ball or a light bulb. They then move on to another store where these things

---

16 *Delinquent Boys: The Culture of the Gang* (Glencoe: The Free Press, 1955).

are covertly exchanged for like articles. Then they move on to other stores to continue the game indefinitely. They steal a basket of peaches, desultorily munch on a few of them and leave the rest to spoil. They steal clothes they cannot wear and toys they will not use. Unquestionably, most delinquents are from the more "needy" and "underprivileged" classes, and unquestionably many things are stolen because they are intrinsically valued. However, a human and compassionate regard for their economic disabilities should not blind us to the fact that stealing is not merely an alternative means to the acquisition of objects otherwise difficult of attainment.

Cohen, Lawrence
Felson, Marcus
"The Minimal Elements of Direct-Contact Predatory Violations" [17]

As we previously stated, despite their great diversity, direct-contact predatory violations share some important requirements which facilitate analysis of their structure. Each successfully completed violation minimally requires an *offender* with both criminal inclinations and the ability to carry out those inclinations, a person or object providing a *suitable target* for the offender, and *absence of guardians* capable of preventing violations. We emphasize that the lack of any one of these elements normally is sufficient to prevent such violations from occurring. Though guardianship is implicit in everyday life, it usually is marked by the absence of violations; hence it is easy to overlook. While police action is analyzed widely, guardianship by ordinary citizens of one another and of property may be one of the most neglected elements in sociological research on crime, especially since it links seemingly unrelated social roles and relationships to the occurrence or absence of illegal acts.

The conjunction of these minimal elements can be used to assess how social structure may affect the tempo of each type of violation. That is, the probability that a violation will occur at any specific time and place might be taken as a function of the convergence of likely offenders and suitable targets in the absence of capable guardians.

---

17 "Social Change and Crime Rate Trends: A Routine Activity Approach," *American Sociological Review* 44, no. 4 (August 1979): 588-608.

Through consideration of how trends and fluctuations in social conditions affect the frequency of this convergence of criminogenic circumstances, an explanation of temporal trends in crime rates can be constructed.

Cohen, Stanley
Deviance and Moral Panic[18]

Societies appear to be subject, every now and then, to periods of moral panic. A condition, episode, person or group of persons emerges to become defined as a threat to societal values and interests; its nature is presented in a stylized and stereotypical fashion by the mass media; the moral barricades are manned by editors, bishops, politicians and other right-thinking people; socially accredited experts pronounce their diagnoses and solutions; ways of coping are evolved or (more often) resorted to; the condition then disappears, submerges or deteriorates and becomes more visible. Sometimes the object of the panic is quite novel and at other times it is something which has been in existence long enough, but suddenly appears in the limelight. Sometimes the panic passes over and is forgotten, except in folklore and collective memory; at other times it has more serious and long-lasting repercussions and might produce such changes as those in legal and social policy or even in the way the society conceives itself.

One of the most recurrent types of moral panic in Britain since the war has been associated with the emergence of various forms of youth culture (originally almost exclusively working class, but often recently middle class or student based) whose behaviour is deviant or delinquent. To a greater or lesser degree, these cultures have been associated with violence. The Teddy Boys, the Mods and Rockers, the Hells Angels, the skinheads and the hippies

---

18 *Folk Devils and Moral Panic: The Creation of the Mods and Rockers* (London: MacGibbon and Kee, 1972).

have all been phenomena of this kind. There have been parallel reactions to the drug problem, student militancy, political demonstrations, football hooliganism, vandalism of various kinds and crime and violence in general. But groups such as the Teddy Boys and the Mods and Rockers have been distinctive in being identified not just in terms of particular events (such as demonstrations) or particular disapproved forms of behaviour (such as drug-taking or violence) but as distinguishable social types. In the gallery of types that society erects to show its members which roles should be avoided and which should be emulated, these groups have occupied a constant position as folk devils: visible reminders of what we should not be. The identities of such social types are public property and these particular adolescent groups have symbolized— both in what they were and how they were reacted to—much of the social change which has taken place in Britain over the last twenty years.

Clarke, Ronald V.
"The Technologies of Situational Crime Prevention"[19]

When it comes to prevention, criminologists generally focus on measures designed to reduce criminal motivation (such as increased welfare aid, educational programs, improved leisure facilities and job opportunities). Offending, however, is as much the result of the emergence of an opportunity as the motivation of its perpetrator, and the most recent theories have therefore considered the role of opportunity in offending. One of the most important approaches among these theories is that of "routine activity," which aims to explain how the physical and social environment of our society creates opportunities for offending by bringing together, in time and space, three key components: a "likely" offender, a "suitable" target, and the absence of "sufficient deterrence."

[...]

Another "opportunity" theory is "rational choice" theory, according to which offending is a deliberate act designed to benefit its perpetrator. In general, for the offender, committing an offense is simply a way to obtain what he desires, whether this is money, peer approval, excitement, sexual gratification, or power over others. In choosing an illegal path, the offender weighs up the effort and risk involved in the offense and the benefit derived from it, with what it would cost to obtain the same thing by legal means. This process of decision-making is often rather rudimentary, but its object is nevertheless

---

19   "Les Technologies de la prévention situationelle," *Les Cahiers de la Sécurité Intérieure* 21 (1995): 101-113.

to bring the offender what he desires at a minimum cost. In parallel with the development of these theories, other approaches aiming to reduce opportunities for offending have been studied, such as "defensible space" or "crime prevention through better environmental design," a "policing policy focused on eliminating problems" and "situational crime prevention."

Cressey, Donald
"Research Implications of Conflicting Conceptions of Victimology"[20]

The Greek 'o' and 'l-o-g-y' in victimology suggest a special branch of science. In turn, the implied scientific character of victimology suggests a focus on problems that are researchable by empirical methods. It seems timely to examine this and alternative conceptions of victimology.

Victimology is not a scientific discipline. Neither is it an academic field (like criminology or ecology) to which scholars and scientists trained in various disciplines make theoretical and research contributions. It is, instead, a non-academic programme under which a hodgepodge of ideas, interests, ideologies and research methods have been rather arbitrarily grouped. Indeed, it is possible that the originator of the word "victimology," Benjamin Mendelsohn, invented the term not because either a scientific discipline or a scientific orientation was present, but because "victimology" was easy to say. As I have elsewhere noted, the word rolls trippingly off the tongue, even as it obscures conflicting concerns for victims, only some of which are scientific.

More specifically, victimology is characterized by a clash between two equally desirable orientations to human suffering—the humanistic and the scientific. This conflict is unseen by some victimologists and rarely mentioned by others. Nevertheless, it seems to interfere with both the humanitarian and the scientific efforts on be-

---

20 "Research Implications of Conflicting Conceptions of Victimology," in *Towards a Critical Victimology,* ed. Ezzat A. Fattah (Basingstoke: Palgrave Macmillan, 1992), 57-73.

half of victims. The humanists' work tends to be depre-
cated because it is considered propagandistic rather than
scientific, and the scientists' work tends to be deprecat-
ed because it is not sufficiently oriented to social action.
Each set of victimologists probably would be better off
if it divorced the other and formed alliances outside the
shadow of the victimology umbrella.

Cusson, Maurice
Why Punish[21]

Safety is the absence of danger and the peace of mind that results from this. The public enjoys safety when it feels relatively sheltered from crime. Security is linked to a low level of attacks on life and people's goods; this is its objective dimension. From this stems a feeling of peace and assurance; this is its subjective dimension.

Safety is not only one of the fundamental objectives of criminal law, but lies at the very heart of the contract that binds citizens to the state. According to Freud, the essential purpose of politics is to protect members of a group from inner or external dangers.

This objective is realized by preventing citizens from resorting to violence against one another and by ensuring the safety of all from external attack. The members of a political group expect their government to ensure above all that their person and goods are not exposed to violence of any kind. The power that shows itself incapable of guaranteeing the safety of its principals will be unable to maintain their allegiance for very long.

There is no need to extol the benefits of safety ad infinitum. It is essential to developing the social fabric without which human beings are unable to truly exist. In the absence of safety, freedom and prosperity remain inaccessible goods. One must be sheltered from violence in order to maintain secure trade with one's fellows.

---

21 *Pourquoi Punir* (Paris: Dalloz, 1987).

d

De Greeff, Étienne
Introduction to Criminology [22] *(1946)*

The failure of simplistic anthropological notions forced researchers to return to personality. A failure of the same kind awaited the over-naive positivism of the sociologists. It might appear an unanswerable argument to show the existence of parallel curves and a high correlation between the price of bread and theft, between the price of cotton and the rate of lynchings, and between the turn of the seasons and the number of homicides and suicides. These facts speak for themselves and are highly significant, without the need to introduce individual will. In effect, say the sociologists, or at least some of them, as a result of the close, regular, and proportional links that have been established between economic and criminal facts, as a result of the permanent coefficient that joins them, it is clear that if individual will has played a role, it has not been an effective one, as the correlations have always remained the same; and thus it may be ignored.

It thus becomes entirely possible to explain the career of an offender solely as a result of the circumstances in which he has found himself; and to explain criminality by a series of economic, geographical, family, and meteorological factors, as long as one never finds oneself faced with a real offender. The question that arises, however, in

22 *Introduction à la Criminologie* (Brussels: Joseph Vandenplan, 1946

145

a case chosen for example from a series of thieves who apparently fell victim to the wartime price of bread, is why certain individuals succumbed to the economic phenomenon.

[...]

We have unduly forgotten that the criminal is above all a human being who resembles other human beings more than he differs from them; that he is not a passive object, an unconscious automaton tossed on the waves of heredity, endocrinology, and social circumstances, and led to crime like Vaucanson's mechanical snake. Like other men, the criminal builds and runs his life, makes and corrects mistakes, and experiences joy and suffering; like other men, he is unaware of the secret influences exerted over his choices by healthy or unhealthy factors; like those of other men his decisions and actions represent what he was best able to do in the given circumstances.

The story of his crime and the story of his life are above all works of humanity. And we will make no real progress as long as, limiting ourselves to listing the causes involved, we do not succeed in gathering these scattered materials into a stable and acceptable whole: a reconstruction of the subject's mental life, a reconstitution of his inner world that can be linked to known facts.

Durkheim, Émile

The Rules of Sociological Method[23] *(1894)*

We observe that certain actions exist which all possess the one external characteristic that, once they have taken place, they provoke on the part of society that special reaction known as punishment. We constitute them as a group sui generis and classify them under a single heading: any action that is punished is termed a crime and we make crime, so defined, the subject matter of a special science of criminology.

[...]

If there is a fact whose pathological nature appears indisputable, it is crime. All criminologists agree on this score. Although they explain this pathology differently, they none the less unanimously acknowledge it. However, the problem needs to be treated less summarily.

Let us in fact apply the rules previously laid down. Crime is not only observed in most societies of a particular species, but in all societies of all types. There is not one in which criminality does not exist, although it changes in form and the actions which are termed criminal are not everywhere the same. Yet everywhere and always there have been men who have conducted themselves in such a way as to bring down punishment upon their heads. If at least, as societies pass from lower to higher types, the crime rate (the relationship between the annual crime figures and population figures) tended to fall, we might believe that, although still remaining a normal phenome-

---

23   *The Rules of Sociological Method,* trans. W.D. Halls (New York: The Free Press, 1982).

non, crime tended to lose that character of normality. Yet there is no single ground for believing such a regression to be real. Many facts would rather seem to point to the existence of a movement in the opposite direction. From the beginning of the century statistics provide us with a means of following the progression of criminality. It has everywhere increased, and in France the increase is of the order of 300 per cent. Thus there is no phenomenon which represents more incontrovertibly all the symptoms of normality, since it appears to be closely bound up with the conditions of all collective life. To make crime a social illness would be to concede that sickness is not something accidental, but on the contrary derives in certain cases from the fundamental constitution of the living creature. This would be to erase any distinction between the physiological and the pathological. It can certainly happen that crime itself has normal forms; this is what happens, for instance, when it reaches an excessively high level. There is no doubt that this excessiveness is pathological in nature. What is normal is simply that criminality exists, provided that for each social type it does not reach or go beyond a certain level which it is perhaps not impossible to fix in conformity with the previous rules.

We are faced with a conclusion which is apparently somewhat paradoxical. Let us make no mistake: to classify crime among the phenomena of normal sociology is not merely to declare that it is an inevitable though regrettable phenomenon arising from the incorrigible wickedness of men; it is to assert that it is a factor in public health, an integrative element in any healthy society. At first sight this result is so surprising that it disconcerted even ourselves for a long time. However, once that first impression of surprise has been overcome it is not difficult to discover reasons to explain this normality and at the same time to confirm it.

[...]

From this viewpoint the fundamental facts of criminology appear to us in an entirely new light. Contrary to current ideas, the criminal no longer appears as an utterly unsociable creature, a sort of parasitic element, a foreign, unassimilable body introduced into the bosom of society. He plays a normal role in social life. For its part, crime must no longer be conceived of as an evil which cannot be circumscribed closely enough. Far from there being cause for congratulation when it drops too noticeably below the normal level, this apparent progress assuredly coincides with and is linked to some social disturbance. Thus the number of crimes of assault never falls so low as it does in times of scarcity. Consequently, at the same time, and as a reaction, the theory of punishment is revised, or rather should be revised. If in fact crime is a sickness, punishment is the cure for it and cannot be 'conceived of otherwise; thus all the discussion aroused revolves round knowing what punishment should be to fulfil its role as a remedy. But if crime is in no way pathological, the object of punishment cannot be to cure it and its true function must be sought elsewhere.

e

Eysenck, Hans Jürgen
Gudjonsson, Gisli H.
The Causes and Cures of Criminality[24]

We have already noted the major dimensions of personality in its noncognitive aspects that according to theory are related to criminality. The general theory concerning this relationship has been developed by J. H. Eysenck (1977). [...] According to this theory, criminality and antisocial conduct are positively and causally related to high psychoticism, high extraversion, and high neuroticism. Here let us merely note that the theory posits biologically determined low degrees of arousal and arousability in extraverts and possibly also in persons high on the psychoticism scale. These lead to behaviors (risk taking, sensation seeking, impulsivity, etc.) that increase the cortical level of arousal to a more acceptable amount. Behaviors of this type do not necessarily lead to actual antisocial behavior; they may also lead to participation in sports, adventure, and other arousal-producing activities. Neuroticism-anxiety, as in the Hullian system, acts as a drive that multiplies with the learned behavior patterns based on this biological foundation and in such a way as to increase the antisocial behavior produced by the P and E personality traits.

[...]

However, one further important aspect of the theory must be mentioned, namely that linking introversion

---

24   *The Causes and Cures of Criminality* (New York: Springer, 1989).

with ease and speed of Pavlovian conditioning (H. J. Eysenck, 1967, 1981). According to this theory, prosocial conduct has to be *learned* by the growing child, and this learning is accomplished through a process of Pavlovian conditioning. Prosocial conduct is praised, antisocial conduct is punished by peers, parents, teachers, and others, and through a thousandfold repetition of such reinforcements, "conscience" becomes established as a conditioned response, leading to prosocial and altruistic behavior. As introverts form conditioned responses of this type more readily than extraverts, they are more easily socialized through Pavlovian conditioning and hence are less likely to indulge in antisocial activities.

f

Fattah, Ezzat

"Victimology: Between Epistemological Criticism and Ideological Attack"[25]

Early studies in victimology were characterized by an almost exclusive preoccupation with victimogenic predispositions, the causal role of the victim, and modeling the relationship between criminals and victims. However, with the exception of a few cases in which the victim is a direct catalyst for the crime, discovering a primary or secondary relationship between the criminal and his victim is often of little value in explaining the motivation or actions of the two parties. Modern victimology has expanded the interpersonal perspective of a simple typology of relations into study of the reciprocal attitudes of the criminal and the victim, and their perceptions of each other. This constitutes one of the most important theoretical developments of recent years. It has not only opened new avenues in the study of offender-victim interactions, but has also provided a new approach to understanding the dynamics of criminal behavior and the entry into criminality. Moreover, research in this area will undoubtedly have major applications in the fields of prevention, rehabilitation, education, and victim therapy. This is a very rich and very broad area. I will limit myself to highlighting a few salient points taken from recent research:

---

25 "La victimologie: entre les critiques épistémologiques et les attaques idéologiques," *Déviance et Société* 5, no. 1 (1981): 71-92.

- Victimology studies appear to indicate that all societies, by stigmatizing certain individuals or certain groups, legitimize their victimization and implicitly or explicitly label them as appropriate targets for criminal attacks.

- Victimology studies indicate that offenders generally make subtle distinctions between suitable targets and unsuitable targets for victimization. They appear to draw a fairly clear dividing line between those who can and those who cannot become victims.

- Offenders appear to have stereotyped definitions and generally agreed images of victims.

- Among the techniques often used by offenders to neutralize moral resistance, overcome inhibitions, and silence their conscience, several use the victim as an agent of legitimization or neutralization. The negation or reification, denigration, exemption, devaluing or deindividualization of the victim are key mechanisms in the process of desensitization, as they lead to the weakening of internal constraints and produce a reduced sense of guilt and diminished dissonance following the assault.

- The previously-established guilt of the victim (whether this guilt is real or imagined by the offender, and whether it is engendered by the actions of the victim or simply by association) appears to almost completely rid the potential offender of all sense of guilt and to provide his conscience with a perfect alibi.

- Laboratory studies, including Milgram's well-known experiments, have confirmed the hypothesis that the closer one brings the victim to the subject (by making him more prominent, more visible, and thus increasing the subject's awareness of his suffering and distress), the more the subject's performance is regulated and the more his obedience to the person conducting the experience is reduced. Empathy for the victim and greater awareness of his suffering appear to constitute inhibiting and controlling forces.

- In certain cases of kidnapping, hostage taking, and aircraft hijacking, particularly where they have lasted for several days or weeks, it has been observed that some victims react to their captors with a positive rather than negative emotional response. This initial favorable reaction can even develop into an emotional attachment or affectional bond. This strange phenomenon, known as "Stockholm Syndrome," has generated several explanations. Some theorists believe that this realignment of affection is produced by the state of dependency that develops between the hostage and his abductor. Others explain Stockholm Syndrome with reference to the Freudian concept of "identification with the aggressor." A third point of view emphasizes the importance of the strong feelings of gratitude felt by the survivor to the abductor for having spared his life.

Ferri, Enrico
Criminal Sociology [26]

[...] the positive criminal school does not consist, as it seems convenient for many of its critics to feign to believe, only in the anthropological study of the criminal; it constitutes a complete renovation,—a radical change of scientific method in the study of criminal social pathology and in the study of what is most effectual among the social and juridical remedies that social pathology presents. The science of crimes and punishments was formerly a doctrinal exposition of the syllogisms brought forth by the sole force of logical fantasy. Our school has made of it a science of positive observation, which, based on anthropology, psychology, and criminal statistics as well as on criminal law and studies relative to imprisonment, becomes the synthetic science to which I myself gave the name "criminal sociology." So that this science, applying the positive method to the study of crime, delinquency and the environment in which they are manifested, only gives to classical criminal science the life-giving breath of the sublime and irrefragable discoveries made in the science of man and society, reconstructed by the doctrine of evolution.

[...]

And it is with these discoveries, intimately concerning man, that the criminologist of today must occupy himself, in order to seek from the experimental sciences, a positive base for his juridical and social conceptions,

---

26 *Criminal Sociology*, trans. Joseph I. Kelly and John Lisle (Boston: Little, Brown, and Company, 1917), chapter III.

unless he consents to resign himself to that mere exercise of rhetoric to which daily practice in the criminal courts gives the lie. The juridical valuation of criminal acts strictly concerns the criminologist. There are two main reasons why he can no longer put off considering it. The first is to prevent laymen drawing extravagant and erroneous conclusions from the facts which belie the old theories; the second, that while the other juridical sciences are concerned with social relations (abstracting individual particularities which do not directly change their value)—the doctrine of crimes and punishment, unlike them, has man, as he really lives and acts in the social medium, as its immediate object.

[...]

Now in recapitulating the most serious and most flagrant divergences between the new results of the positive sciences (which study man as a physio-psychic organism, bom and living in the midst of a fixed physical and social medium) and the metaphysical doctrines on crime punishment and penal justice of the past, I think I can reduce them to the following points.

Among the fundamental bases of criminal and penal law as heretofore understood are these three postulates:

1. The criminal has the same ideas, the same sentiments as any other man.

2. The principal effect of punishment is to arrest the excess and the increase of crime.

3. Man is endowed with free will or moral liberty; and for that reason, is morally guilty and legally responsible for his crimes.

On the other hand, one has only to go out of the scholastic circle of juridical studies and "a priori" affirmations, to find in opposition to the preceding assertions, these conclusions of the experimental sciences:

1. Anthropology shows by facts that the delinquent is not a normal man; that on the contrary he represents a special class, a variation of the human race through organic and psychical abnormalities, either hereditary or acquired.

2. Statistics prove that the appearance, increase, decrease, or disappearance of crime depends upon other reasons than the punishments prescribed by the codes and applied by the courts.

3. Positive psychology has demonstrated that the pretended free will is a purely subjective illusion.

Foucault, Michel
Discipline and Punish[27]

The penitentiary technique and the delinquent are in a sense twin brothers. It is not true that it was the discovery of the delinquent through a scientific rationality that introduced into our old prisons the refinement of penitentiary techniques. Nor is it true that the internal elaboration of penitentiary methods has finally brought to light the "objective" existence of a delinquency that the abstraction and rigidity of the law were unable to perceive. They appeared together, the one extending from the other, as a technological ensemble that forms and fragments the object to which it applies its instruments. And it is this delinquency, formed in the foundations of the judicial apparatus, among the *"basses oeuvres,"* the servile tasks, from which justice averts its gaze, out of the shame it feels in punishing those it condemns, it is this delinquency that now comes to haunt the untroubled courts and the majesty of the laws; it is this delinquency that must be known, assessed, measured, diagnosed, treated when sentences are passed. It is now this delinquency, this anomaly, this deviation, this potential danger, this illness, this form of existence, that must be taken into account when the codes are rewritten. Delinquency is the vengeance of the prison on justice. It is a revenge formidable enough to leave the judge speechless. It is at this point that the criminologists raise their voices.

But we must not forget that the prison, that concentrated and austere figure of all the disciplines, is not an endog-

---

27   *Discipline and Punish,* trans. Alan Sheridan (London: Penguin, 1977).

enous element in the penal system as defined at the turn of the eighteenth and nineteenth centuries. The theme of a punitive society and of a general semio-technique of punishment that has sustained the "ideological" codes—Beccarian or Benthamite—did not itself give rise to the universal use of the prison. This prison came from else-where— from the mechanisms proper to a disciplinary power. Now, despite this heterogeneity, the mechanisms and effects of the prison have spread right through mod-ern criminal justice; delinquency and the delinquents have become parasites on it through and through. One must seek the reason for this formidable "efficiency" of the prison. But one thing may be noted at the outset: the penal justice defined in the eighteenth century by the reformers traced two possible but divergent lines of objectification of the criminal: the first was the series of "monsters," moral or political, who had fallen outside the social pact; the second was that of the juridical subject re-habilitated by punishment. Now the "delinquent" makes it possible to join the two lines and to constitute under the authority of medicine, psychology or criminology, an individual in whom the offender of the law and the object of a scientific technique are superimposed—or almost—one upon the other. That the grip of the pris-on on the penal system should not have led to a violent reaction of rejection is no doubt due to many reasons. One of these is that, in fabricating delinquency, it gave to criminal justice a unitary field of objects, authenticated by the "sciences," and thus enabled it to function on a general horizon of "truth."

g

Gall, Franz Josef
On the Functions of the Brain and of Each of Its Parts (1825) [28]

The object of all my researches is to found a doctrine on the functions of the brain. The result of this doctrine ought to be the development of a perfect knowledge of human nature.

The possibility of any doctrine, in relation to the moral and intellectual function of the brain, supposes:

1. That moral and intellectual faculties are innate.

2. That their exercise or manifestation depends on organization.

3. That the brain is the organ of all the propensities, sentiments, and faculties.

4. That the brain is composed of as many particular organs as there are propensities, sentiments, and faculties, which differ essentially from each other.

And as the organs and their localities can be determined by observation only, it is also necessary that the form of the head or cranium should represent, in most cases, the form of the brain, and should suggest various means to ascertain the fundamental qualities and faculties, and the seat of their organs.

---

28 *On the Functions of the Brain and of Each of Its Parts,* trans. Winslow Lewis (New York: Marsh, Capen & Lyon, 1835).

Galton, Francis
"Finger Prints"[29]

1. The art of taking clear impressions of the fingers, with the use of printing ink, is quickly learnt; jailers in all English prisons, for example, are now able to take excellent prints. Those studying the area should however observe the operation before attempting to practice it. It requires only a very simple set of printing tools.

2. The patterns formed by the papillary ridges that adorn the tips of the fingers are constant throughout a person's life. The remarkable consistency in their appearance applies not only to their general form, but to the numerous details specific to each individual pattern, such as the "bifurcations," "islands," and "enclosures," of which there are around thirty in the pattern of each finger and which never change.

3. Cuts and scars do not destroy the legibility of these patterns except in extreme cases; their existence can even assist identification.

4. Using the classification method adopted in my experimental collection, a series of 2,500 finger prints, it is easy to retrieve any one specimen. On each occasion the prints of the ten fingers of an individual were submitted to our examination, it was easy for either myself or my assistant to ascertain whether another print of the same hands, taken at an earlier period, was already

---

29 "Les empreintes digitales," *Archives d'Anthropologie Criminelle, de Criminologie et de Psychologie Normale et Pathologique* 10 (1895).

present in the collection. This was achieved either by returning to the cards on which the prints had been taken, or by reference to the catalogue in which we had placed the "index-headings" in alphabetical order, by which means it is possible to distinguish between different series of prints.

5. he index-headings mentioned above are obtained by classifying the pattern of each finger, taken separately, in one of four basic classes—A, R, U, and W—and also on occasion by counting the ridges (see 8) and by using descriptive suffixes (see 8).

6. The relative frequency with which the patterns occur in the different classes is such that for every thirteen index finger patterns we will find on average two specimens of A, three cases of R, four cases of U, and four cases of W. The proportions are not the same for the other fingers.

7. A (Arches). Here the papillary ridges cross the finger in straight lines on and beside the final joint. From there, as they approach the end of the finger, they become more and more arched. This arrangement constitutes a continuous system in which no ridge turns back on itself.

8. Classes R and U can be easily subdivided by counting the number of ridges that would cross an imaginary line drawn from the delta to the core. The ridges can be easily and accurately counted with appropriate optical equipment. Having practiced together until we were in agreement on the precise termini (outlined

in detail in my book), my assistant and I rarely differed by more than one or two ridges across a long series of experiments, and when we did differ it was generally possible to foresee the nature and difference of such variance. The number of ridges between the termini of the index varies from one to over twenty, and the relative frequency of each number of ridges between three and fifteen is approximately the same. The R and U sections can therefore be considerably subdivided by counting the ridges. We have succeeded in subdividing the W class by counting from the outer delta to the core or, if there are two cores in the pattern, to that which is closest.

9. The final item to note is the system of suffixes, which provides useful indications for the particular features of the pattern.

Garofalo, Raffaele
Criminology: Studying the Nature of Crime and the Theory of Punishment [30]

Toward the close of the 1800s the study of the criminal from the point of view of the natural sciences began to engage marked attention. As a result, his anthropologic and psychologic descriptions have been noted; he has been presented as a type, as a variety of the "genus homo." But when we come to consider how this theory may be applied to legislation, serious difficulties are encountered. By no means every person who is an offender according to legal standards answers the description of the naturalists' criminal man—a circumstance which has thrown doubt upon the practical value of such studies. Nor could the case be otherwise, from the very fact that although the naturalists speak of the *criminal*, they have omitted to tell us what they understand by the word *crime*. This task of definition they have left to the jurists, without attempting to say whether or not criminality from the legal standpoint is coterminous with criminality from the sociologic point of view. It is this lack of definition which has hitherto rendered the naturalists' study of crime a thing apart and caused it to be regarded as a matter of purely scientific interest with which legislation has nothing to do.

To my mind, then, the initial step in our investigation should be the attainment of the sociologic notion of crime. It will not do to say that we are dealing with a legal notion and that consequently its definition belongs

---

30 *Criminology*, trans. Robert Wyness Millar (Boston: Little, Brown & Company, 1914).

to the jurists alone. We are here concerned not with a technical term, but with a word which expresses an idea accessible to every one, irrespective of his knowledge of the law. The law-maker has not created this term, but has borrowed it from the popular language. He has not even defined it. All that he has done is to group a certain number of acts and call them crimes. This is why, at the same period of time and often within the confines of a single nation, we find a given act in one locality treated as a crime and in another not punished at all. It follows that the legal classification can in no way foreclose sociologic investigation. For the solution of his doubts regarding the boundaries of criminality, the sociologist cannot turn to the man of law, as he would to the chemist to learn the nature of salts or acid, or to the physicist to be informed of the notion of light or electricity. This notion of crime he must seek for himself. Only when he will have taken the pains to tell us what he understands by crime, shall we know what criminals he is talking about. In a word, we must arrive at the notion of the *natural crime*.

[...]

But if we thus are compelled to relinquish the idea of collecting a group of *facts* universally hated and punished, it by no means follows that the notion of the natural crime is impossible of achievement. To attain it, however, we must change method: we must lay aside the analysis of *facts* and undertake that of *sentiments*. Crime, in reality, is always a harmful action, but, at the same time, an action which wounds some one of the sentiments which, by common consent, are called the moral sense of a human aggregation. Now, the moral sense has developed but slowly: it has varied and continues to vary according to circumstances of race and time. Each of the sentiments of which it is composed has from time to time undergone perceptible augmentation or diminution of strength. Hence it is that there exist wide differences in ideas of morality, and as a necessary result, differences not less considerable in this species of immorality without which no harmful action can ever be regarded as a crime. We must endeavor, then, to ascertain whether, in spite of the lack of uniformity in the emotions excited by acts differently appreciated by different aggregations, there is not a constant character in the emotions aroused by acts which are appreciated in an identical manner,— in other words, whether the difference is not one of form rather than of substance. Reference to the evolution of the moral sense can alone throw light on this question.

Glueck, Sheldon and Eleanor
Delinquents in the Making[31]

By and large, examination of existing researches in juvenile delinquency discloses a tendency to overemphasize a particular approach or explanation. Proponents of various theories of causation still too often insist that the truth is to be found only in their own special fields of study and that, *ex hypothesi,* researches made by those working in other disciplines can contribute little to the understanding and management of the crime problem.

Yet it stands to reason that, since so little is as yet known about the intricacies of normal human behavior, it is the better part of wisdom not to be overawed by any branch of science or methodology to the neglect of other promising leads in the study of aberrant behavior. When, therefore, research into the causes of delinquency emphasizes the sociologic, or ecologic, or cultural, or psychiatric, or psychoanalytic, or anthropologic approach, relegating the others to a remote position, if not totally ignoring them, we must immediately be on guard. The problems of human motivation and behavior involve the study of man as well as society, of nature as well as nurture, of segments or "mechanisms" of the human mind as well as the total personality, of patterns of intimate social activity as well as larger areas of social process or masses of culture. They must, therefore, be studies through *the participation of several disciplines.*

---

31   *Delinquents in the Making: Paths to Prevention* (New York: Harper, 1952).

Goffman, Erving
Asylums: Essays on the Social Situation of Mental Patients and Other Inmates[32]

A total institution may be defined as a place of residence and work where a large number of like-situated individuals, cut off from the wider society for an appreciable period of time, together lead an enclosed, formally administered round of life.

[...]

A basic social arrangement in modern society is that the individual tends to sleep, play, and work in different places, with different co-participants, under different authorities, and without an overall rational plan. The central feature of total institutions can be described as a breakdown of the barriers ordinarily separating these three spheres of life. [...]

The handling of many human needs by the bureaucratic organization of whole blocks of people—whether or not this is a necessary or effective means of social organization in the circumstances—is the key fact of total institutions.

---

32 Asylums: Essays on the Social Situation of Mental Patients and Other Inmates (New York: Anchor Books, 1961).

Gottfredson, Michael R.
Hirschi, Travis
A General Theory of Crime [33]

The decision to ascribe stable individual differences in criminal behavior to self-control was made only after considering several alternatives, one of which (criminality) has been used before (Hirschi and Gottfredson, 1986). A major consideration was consistency between the classical conception of crime and this alternative conception of the criminal. It seemed unwise to try to integrate a choice theory of crime with a deterministic image of the offender, especially when such integration was unnecessary. In fact, the compatibility of the classical view of crime and the idea that people differ in self-control seems remarkable. Classical theory is a theory of social or external control, a theory based on the idea that the costs of crime depend on the individual's current location in or bond to society. What classical theory lacks is an explicit idea of self-control, the idea that people also differ in the extent to which they are vulnerable to the temptations of the moment. Combining the two ideas thus merely recognizes the simultaneous existence of social and individual restraints on behavior.

An obvious alternative is the concept of criminality. The disadvantages of that concept, however, are numerous. First, it connotes causation or determinism, a positive tendency to crime that is contrary to the classical model and, in this view, contrary to the facts. Whereas self-control suggests that people differ in the extent to which

---

33 *A General Theory of Crime* (Stanford: Stanford University Press, 1990).

they are restrained from criminal acts, criminality suggests that people differ in the extent to which they are compelled to crime. The concept of self-control is thus consistent with the observation that criminals do not require or need crime, and the concept of criminality is inconsistent with this observation. By the same token, the idea of low self-control is compatible with the observation that criminal acts require no special capabilities, needs, or motivation; they are, in this sense, available to everyone. In contrast, the idea of criminality as a special tendency suggests that criminal acts require special people for their performance and enjoyment. Finally, lack of restraint or low self-control allows almost any deviant, criminal, exciting, or dangerous act; in contrast, the idea of criminality covers only a narrow portion of the apparently diverse acts engaged in by people at one end of the dimension now under discussion.

The concept of conscience comes closer than criminality to self-control and is harder to distinguish from it. Unfortunately, that concept has connotations of compulsion (to conformity) not, strictly speaking, consistent with a choice model (or with the operation of conscience). It does not seem to cover the behaviors analogous to crime that appear to be controlled by natural sanctions rather than social or moral sanctions, and in the end it typically refers to how people feel about their acts rather than to the likelihood that they will or will not commit them. Thus, accidents and employment instability are not usually seen as produced by failures of conscience, and writers in the conscience tradition do not typically make the connection between moral and prudent behavior. Finally, conscience is used primarily to summarize the results of learning via negative reinforcement, and even those favorably disposed to its use have little more to say about it(see, e.g., Eysenck, 1977; Wilson and Herrnstein, 1985).

It is now possible to describe the nature of self-control, the individual characteristic relevant to the commission of criminal acts. Assuming that the nature of this characteristic can be derived directly from the nature of criminal acts, it can thus be inferred from the nature of crime what people who refrain from criminal acts are like before they reach the age at which crime becomes a logical possibility. One can then work back further to the factors producing their restraint, back to the causes of self-control. In this view, lack of self-control does not require crime and can be counteracted by situational conditions or other properties of the individual. At the same time, it seems that high self-control effectively reduces the possibility of crime—that is, those possessing it will be substantially less likely at all periods of life to engage in criminal acts.

Guerry, André-Michel
Essay on the Moral Statistics of France [34]

In criminal matters, it was said, just as in those pertaining to the moral sciences, the facts are too changeable, too hard to pin down, to be captured by numerical observation. Thus, so the argument went, it was necessary to restrict oneself, as in the past, to theories based on logical reasoning, to the examination of general concepts, and to individual experience. Nonetheless, we might ask how the results of personal experience are to be evaluated, since they are neither classified nor stated numerically, and, as a consequence, the importance of particular experiences varies, not only from one individual to another, but even within individuals themselves. Facts of a particular type momentarily produce the most vivid and durable impressions on one's mind depending on one's biases and the special or accidental circumstances under which the experience occurs. How is one to pull together such disparate elements and compare them with one another? Indeed, what is a general concept? It is a collection, a categorization, of particular facts of which it is nothing but the simplest expression and whose enumeration it implies. If particular facts have not first been observed and established as fact, or if they are incomplete, vague, uncertain, or unknown, what would the general concept represent? Clearly, each person could create such a generalization, modify it at will, and thereby lay the foundation for any theoretical system one could imagine.

Moreover, if prevailing opinion (based on this kind of general experience) about a great number of already rig-

---

34 *Essay on the Moral Statistics of France*, trans. Hugh P. Whitt and Victor W. Reinking (Lewiston: The Edwin Mellen Press, 2002).

orously established facts of moral statistics were entirely mistaken—and the remainder of this work will prove that this is the case—is it possible to assume that this conventional wisdom would be any less erroneous when based on facts which are less directly observed and consequently more difficult to analyze?

[...]

Criminal statistics becomes as empirical and accurate as the other observational sciences when one restricts oneself to the best-observed facts and groups them in such a way as to minimize accidental variation. General patterns then appear with such great regularity that it is impossible to attribute them to random chance. Each year sees the same number of crimes in the same order reproduced in the same region. Each type of crime has its particular invariant distribution by sex, by age, and by season of the year. All these are accompanied in parallel fashion by secondary patterns which appear less important and whose regularities are very difficult to explain.

[...]

If we were now to consider the infinite number of circumstances which might lead to the commission of a crime, the outside influences or purely personal factors which determine the character of individuals, we would find it difficult to conceive that, in the final analysis, their interplay should lead to such constant effects, that acts of free will should develop into a fixed pattern, varying within such narrow limits. We would be forced to recognize that the facts of the moral order, like those of the physical order, obey invariant laws, and that, in many respect, the judicial statistics render this a virtual certainty.

Also, despite the fact that statistics has sometimes been abused, and despite the critical responses by writers whose theories it contradicts, moral statistics has imparted, on all sides, a new direction to studies with relevance for penal legislation and public morals. Regardless of what opinion or what theoretical system one may wish to attack or defend on these matters, henceforth one will no longer be able to scorn the help offered by statistics; it will be necessary to pay attention to the facts presented by statistics and to discuss them.

h

Hirschi, Travis
Causes of Delinquency [35]

Control theories assume that delinquent acts result when an individual's bond to society is weak or broken. Since these theories embrace two highly complex concepts, the *bond* of the individual to *society*, it is not surprising that they have at one time or another formed the basis of explanations of most forms of aberrant or unusual behavior. It is also not surprising that control theories have described the elements of the bond to society in many ways, and that they have focused on a variety of units as the point of control.

I begin with a classification and description of the elements of the bond to conventional society.

[...]

The internalization of norms, conscience, or super-ego thus lies in the attachment of the individual to others.

[...]

Few would deny that men on occasion obey the rules simply from fear of consequences. This rational component in conformity we label commitment. [...] The idea, then, is that the person invests time, energy himself, in a certain line of activity—say, getting an education,

---

35 *Causes of Delinquency* (Berkeley: University of California Press, 1969).

building up a business, acquiring a reputation for virtue. When or whenever he considers deviant behavior, he must consider the costs of this deviant behavior, the risk he runs of losing the investment he has made in conventional behavior. If attachment to others is the sociological counterpart of the superego or conscience, commitment is the counterpart of the ego or common sense.

[...]

Involvement or engrossment in conventional activities is thus often part of a control theory. The assumption, widely shared, is that a person may be simply too busy doing conventional things to find time to engage in deviant behavior. The person involved in conventional activities is tied to appointments, deadlines, working hours, plans, and the like, so the opportunity to commit deviant acts rarely arises. To the extent that he is engrossed in conventional activities he cannot even think about deviant acts, let alone act out his inclinations.

[...]

Unlike the cultural deviance theory, the control theory assumes the existence of a common value system within the society or group whose norms are being violated. If the deviant is committed to a value system different from that of conventional society, there is, within the context of the theory, nothing to explain. The question is, "Why does a man violate the rules in which he believes?" It is not, "Why do men differ in their beliefs about what constitutes good and desirable conduct?" [...] We assume, in contrast, that there is *variation* in the extent to which people believe they should obey the rules of society, and, furthermore, that the less a person believes he should obey the rules, the more likely he is to violate them. [...] The idea of a common (or perhaps better, a single) value system is consistent with the fact, or presumption, of variation in the strength of moral beliefs. We have not suggested that delinquency is based on beliefs counter to conventional morality; we have not suggested that delinquents do not believe delinquent acts are wrong. They may well believe these acts are wrong, but the meaning and efficacy of such beliefs are contingent upon other beliefs and, indeed, on the strength of other ties to the conventional order.

Hulsman, Lodewijk Henri Christiaan (known as Louk)
Bernat de Celis, Jacqueline
"Foundations and Principles of the Theory of Prison Abolition"[36]

Two complementary observations indicate the double foundation of the abolitionist perspective:

1. Far from tackling the problems it is supposed to resolve, the prison system creates new ones: it is a social evil. 2. Parallel conflict resolution mechanisms show that a society without a penal system is already in place before our very eyes. Acknowledging and allowing it to develop would render the prison system quite simply obsolete [...] we must escape the logic of the prison system in order to devise a society from which it has disappeared. The concepts and language of the prison system trap us in its field, and we must make a concerted mental effort to escape from them. When we speak of "crime" or "offending," an image immediately springs to mind, hether we wish it to or not, of a guilty perpetrator. If on the other hand we use the word "event" and the term "situation of conflict" or other such wording with a neutral charge, a space emerges that allows for a range of interpretations. If we replace the terms "offender" and "victim" with the phrase "individuals involved in a problem," we prevent ourselves from mentally fixing these individuals in predetermined roles that limit their freedom of conscience and turn them ipso facto into adversaries. We leave a space free for responses other than those of the punitive

---

36   "Fondements et enjeux de la théorie de l'abolition du système pénal," *Revue de l'Université de Bruxelles* 1, no. 3 (1984): 297-317.

model. It is only when we free ourselves from the penal dialectic that we can escape the cycle of "offending—prison—repeat offending—prison" that the penal logic presents as inevitable. Most importantly, it is only when we cease to regard individuals who fall into the clutches of the system as a separate, subhuman category of society, and when we cease to believe there is no solution other than marginalizing them, that we become able, beyond a concern for "prevention" that harks back to the old Penal Code, to imagine social arrangements capable of making certain undesirable interpersonal problems less frequent or less serious.

k

Katz, Jack
Seductions of Crime: Moral and Sensual Attractions in Doing Evil[37]

The study of crime has been preoccupied with a search for background forces, usually defects in the offenders' psychological backgrounds or social environments, to the neglect of the positive, often wonderful attractions within the lived experience of criminality. The novelty of this book [from which this extract is taken] is its focus on the seductive qualities of crimes: those aspects in the foreground of criminality that make its various forms sensible, even sensually compelling, ways of being.

The social science literature contains only scattered evidence of what it means, feels, sounds, tastes, or looks like to commit a particular crime. Readers of research on homicide and assault do not hear the slaps and curses, see the pushes and shoves, or feel the humiliation and rage that may build toward the attack, sometimes persisting after the victim's death. How adolescents manage to make the shoplifting or vandalism of cheap and commonplace things a thrilling experience has not been intriguing to many students of delinquency. Researchers of adolescent gangs have never grasped why their subjects so often stubbornly refuse to accept the outsider's insistence that they wear the "gang" label. The description of "cold-blooded,

---

37   *Seductions of Crime: Moral and Sensual Attractions in Doing Evil* (New York: Perseus Books Group, 1988).

senseless murders" has been left to writers outside the social sciences. Neither academic methods nor academic theories seem to be able to grasp why such killers may have been courteous to their victims just moments before the killing, why they often wait until they have dominated victims in sealed-off environments before coldly executing them, or how it makes sense to them to kill when only petty cash is at stake. Sociological and psychological studies of robbery rarely focus on the *distinctive* attractions of robbery, even though research has now clearly documented that alternative forms of criminality are available and familiar to many career robbers. In sum, only rarely have sociologists taken up the challenge of explaining the qualities of deviant experience.

Whatever the relevance of antecedent events and contemporaneous social conditions, something causally essential happens in the very moments in which the crime is committed. The assailant must sense, then and there, a distinctive constraint or seductive appeal that he did not sense a little while before in a substantially similar place. Although his economic status, peer group relations, Oedipal conflicts, genetic makeup, internalized machismo, history of child abuse, and the like remains the same, he must suddenly become propelled to commit the crime. Thus, the central problem is to understand the emergence of distinctive sensual dynamics.

To believe that a person can suddenly feel propelled to crime without any independently verifiable change in his background, it seems that we must almost believe in magic. And, indeed, this is precisely what we must do. When they are committing crimes, people feel drawn and propelled to their criminality, but in feeling determined by outside forces, they do nothing morally spe-cial. The particular seductions and compulsions they ex-perience may be unique to crime, but the sense of being seduced and compelled is not. To grasp the magic in the criminal's sensuality, we must acknowledge our own.

Kelling, George
The Kansas City Preventive Patrol Experiment [38]

Ever since the creation of a patrolling force in 13th century Hangchow, preventive patrol by uniformed personnel has been a primary function of policing. [...] Police themselves, the general public, and elected officials have always believed that the presence or potential presence of police officers on patrol severely inhibits criminal activity.

[...]

To the present day, [this] has been the prevailing view. While modern technology, through the creation of new methods of transportation, surveillance and communications, has added vastly to the tools of patrol, and while there have been refinements in patrol strategies based upon advanced probability formulas and other computerized methods, the general principle has remained the same. Today's police recruits, like virtually all those before them, learn from both teacher and textbook that patrol is the "backbone" of police work.

[...]

Challenges to preconceptions about the value of preventive police patrol were exceedingly rare until recent years. When researcher Bruce Smith, writing about patrol in 1930, noted that its effectiveness "lacks scientific demonstration," few paid serious attention.

---

38 George Kelling, Tony Pate, Duane Dieckman, and Charles E. Brown, *The Kansas City Preventive Patrol Experiment* (Washington DC: Police Foundation, 1974).

[...]

It was in this context that the Kansas City, Missouri, Police Department, under a grant from the Police Foundation, undertook in 1972 the most comprehensive experiment ever conducted to analyze the effectiveness of routine preventive patrol.

[...]

The experiment is described in detail later in this summary. Briefly, it involved variations in the level of routine preventive patrol within 15 Kansas City police beats. These beats were randomly divided into three groups. In five "reactive" beats, routine preventive patrol was eliminated and officers were instructed to respond only to calls for service. In five "control" beats routine preventive patrol was maintained at its usual level of one car per beat. In the remaining five "proactive" beats, routine preventive patrol was intensified by two to three times its usual level through the assignment of additional patrol cars and through the frequent presence of cars from the "reactive" beats.

[...]

The experiment found that the three experimental patrol conditions appeared not to affect crime, service delivery and citizen feelings of security in ways the public and the police often assume they do.

For example:

- as revealed in the victimization surveys, the experimental conditions had no significant effect on [...] crimes traditionally considered to be deterrable through preventive patrol;

- in terms of rates of reporting crime to the police, few differences [...] occurred [...];

- in terms of departmental reported crime, only one set of differences across experimental conditions was found and this one was judged likely to have been a random occurrence;

- few significant differences [...]in terms of citizen attitudes toward police services;

- citizen fear of crime, overall, was not affected by experimental conditions;

- there were few differences [...] in the number and types of anti-crime protective measures used by citizens;

- experimental conditions did not appear to significantly affect citizen satisfaction with the police [...];

- experimental conditions had no significant effect on [...] police response time [...];

- although few measures were used to assess the impact of experimental conditions on traffic accidents and injuries, no significant differences were apparent.

1

Lacassagne, Alexandre
"The Progress of Legal Medicine"[39]

As the teaching to which I have dedicated myself for thirty-three years comes to an end, I permit myself to quote you these aphorisms from the Lyon School: any act detrimental to the existence of a group is a crime. All crime is an obstacle to progress. The social environment is the breeding ground of criminality; the microbe is the criminal, an element of no importance until the day he finds the culture plate in which he may thrive. Societies get the criminals they deserve. Such notions can be summarized in the words of Montesquieu: "The means to suppress crime is sentencing; the means to correct behavior is example."

---

39   "Les transformations du droit penal et les progrès de la medicine légale de 1810 à 1912," *Archives d'Anthropologie Criminelle, de Criminologie et de Psychologie Normale et Pathologique* 28 (1913): 321-364.

Lagrange, Hugues
The Denial of Cultures [40]

Urban riots, delinquency, suicide, and the separation of the sexes are spreading across many neighborhoods situated on the periphery of large cities. These phenomena, which particularly involve young people, are, in my opinion, the symptoms of a new social question that has not been considered from all angles. In response to youth offending, we have often rightly focused in France on the effects of unemployment and the decreasing proportion of actively employed men in deprived neighborhoods.

[...]

To explain the persistent offending in these neighborhoods, beyond consideration [...] of the economic and social conditions, two complementary models of interpretation have been put forward in France. The first argues that these areas are the scene of family breakdown and changing solidarities, fed by overly generous welfare policies, and a supposedly widespread crisis of paternal authority, educational permissiveness, and a lack of interest in schooling.

[...]

The second interpretation points to the inward-looking attitude of migrants, particularly those from Africa and Turkey, and focuses on the dangers of a communitarian drift, in which it identifies the seeds of a challenge to common rights and republican values.

---

40 *Le Déni des Cultures* (Paris: Éditions du Seuil, 2010).

[...]

What do the theory of moral decline and the theory of cultural radicalization have in common? In contrast to the first interpretation, I believe that offending in high-immigration neighborhoods is motivated not only by socioeconomic issues but by an excess of authority and a lack of autonomy for women and adolescents. In these neighborhoods, it is not so much a question of the disintegration of the social bond engendered by the phenomenon of "exclusion," but the "over-inclusion" of individuals in the local and various bonds formed by family influences. Whether we like it or not, these difficulties are also related to cultural issues. Does this mean that we should adopt the second interpretation? [...] the model of a return to tradition is also flawed, as it tends to essentialize the culture of origin [...] Although there is certainly today a cultural problem in neighborhoods with high immigration, this is less the result of irredentism to cultures of origin than of the norms and values born from their encounter with host societies. It is the conditions of migratory experience, a complex and often painful encounter woven from conflict and frustrations, that engender a large part of the difficulties.

Landesco, John
Organized Crime in Chicago[41]

Organized vice as a form of law-breaking is more deeply rooted in the social and political order in Chicago than is generally accepted.

The crusades against vice, even when they succeeded in achieving the objectives at which they aimed, as in the abolition of the segregated vice district, do not seem to have extirpated the social evil; they have, however, driven it deeper into the community life, where it tends to find concealed forms of expression.

Indeed, the effects of reforms designed to bring about change may place new opportunities for political corruption in the hands of vice and other law-breaking elements.

Politicians often capitalize public sentiment against an evil and divert it to the purposes of factional politics. Reform becomes a means of winning elections rather than an agency for correcting abuses. Under present conditions, vice lords, gamblers and law-breakers play as active a part in elections as any other element in the community. As they become a part of the political organization that can be relied upon, they invariably exercise an undue influence on the people who represent them in politics. Law enforcement under these circumstances tends to become a sham. Resorts protected by political influence are allowed to run, while other places are repeatedly raided.

---

41 *Organized Crime in Chicago, Illinois Crime Survey*, part III (Chicago: Illinois Association for Criminal Justice, 1929).

Under these conditions the police, whose natural impulse is to enforce the law, become cynical and corrupt.

Every new administration, whether liberal or reform, is likely to disturb the previously existing arrangements between officials and law-breakers. Changes of administration, therefore, tend to inure to the advantage of the abler and more experienced law-breakers. In Chicago, evidence has been presented showing remarkable continuity and persistency of both major and minor personalities in organized vice over a period of twenty-five years. Indeed, there has been something like a royal succession from Colosimo to Torrio, and to Capone.

Finally, with the coming of prohibition, the personnel of organized vice took the lead in the systematic organization of this new and profitable field of exploitation. All this experience gained by years of struggle against reformers and concealed agreements with politicians was brought into service in organizing the production and distribution of beer and whiskey.

Lavater, Johann Caspar
"Physiognomy"[42]

Taking it in its most extensive sense, I use the word physiognomy to signify the exterior, or superficies of man, in motion or at rest, whether viewed in the original or by portrait.

Physiogonomy, or, as more shortly written Physiognomy, is the science or knowledge of the correspondence between the external and internal man, the visible superficies and the invisible contents.

Physiognomy may be divided into the various parts, or views under which man may be considered; that is to say, into the animal, the moral, and the intellectual.

Whoever forms a right judgment of the character of man, from those first impressions which are made by his exterior, is naturally a physiognomist. The scientific physiognomist is he who can arrange, and accurately define, the exterior traits; and the philosophic physiognomist is he who is capable of developing the principles of these exterior traits and tokens, which are the internal causes of external effects.

Physiognomy is properly distinguished from pathognomy.

Physiognomy, opposed to pathognomy, is the knowledge of the signs of the powers and inclinations of men. Pathognomy is the knowledge of the signs of the passions.

---

42 "Physiognomy, Pathognomy," in *Essays on Physiognomy: For the Promotion of the Knowledge and the Love of Mankind*, trans. Thomas Holcroft (London: C. Whittingham, 1804).

Physiognomy, therefore, teaches the knowledge of character at rest; and pathognomy of character in motion.

Character at rest is displayed by the form of the solid and the appearance of the moveable parts, while at rest. Character impassioned is manifested by the moveable parts, in motion.

Physiognomy may be compared to the sum total of the mind; pathognomy to the interest which is the product of this sum total. The former shows what man is in general; the latter what he becomes at particular moments: or, the one what he might be, the other what he is. The first is the root and the stem of the second, the soil in which it is planted. Whoever believes the latter and not the former believes in fruit without a tree, in corn without land.

All people read the countenance pathognomonically; few indeed read it physiognomonically.

Pathognomy has to combat the arts of dissimulation; physiognomy has not.

These two sciences are to the friend of truth inseparable; but as physiognomy is much less studied than pathognomy, I shall chiefly confine myself to the former.

Lecuyer, Bernard-Pierre
"Social Regulation, Social Constraint, and Social Control"[43]

The fundamental concepts of sociology include "social control," as it is termed by English-speaking writers. Its general meaning is well known: essentially it is the overall process that contributes, along with socialization, to ensuring the maintenance and continuity of the social structure. While the general meaning of the concept—albeit with major nuances and divergences—is not in doubt, the same cannot be said for its precise expression in French.

Some authors have resigned themselves to translating it directly into French as "contrôle social," but this solution is satisfactory only if we accept that there is an exact correspondence between "control" and "contrôle"—which is not the case.

[...]

"Social control" is not translated by "contrôle social." The French word "contrôle" includes the meaning of verification, while the English word "control" signifies power, strength, authority, influence, and even suggestion. The generally preferred translation is "régulation sociale" [social regulation], which appears to correspond in a fairly satisfactory fashion to the very large scope of the process (from constraint to influence) included in the term "control." It is also necessary to retain the term "contrainte sociale" [social constraint] as used by Durkheim, at least

---

43 "Régulation sociale, contrainte sociale et 'Social control'," *Revue Française de Sociologie* 8, no. 1 (1967): 78-85.

for that period of his writing in which he clearly distinguished himself from English-speaking theories of "social control" by his primary focus on exteriority and constraint, which in his view characterizes social facts.

Lemert, Edwin M.
"Primary and Secondary Deviation"[44]

From a narrower sociological viewpoint, the deviations are not significant until they are organized subjectively and transformed into active roles and become the social criteria for assigning status. The deviant individuals must react symbolically to their own behavior aberrations and fix them in their sociopsychological patterns. The deviations remain primary deviations or symptomatic and situational as long as they are rationalized or otherwise dealt with as functions of a socially acceptable role. Under such conditions normal and pathological behaviors remain strange and somewhat tensional bedfellows in the same person. Undeniably a vast amount of such segmental and partially integrated pathological behavior exists in our society and has impressed many writers in the field of social pathology.

Just how far and for how long a person may go in dissociating his sociopathic tendencies so that they are merely troublesome adjuncts of normally conceived roles is not known. Perhaps it depends upon the number of alternative definitions of the same overt behavior that he can develop; perhaps certain physiological factors (limits) are also involved. However, if the deviant acts are repetitive and have a high visibility, and if there is a severe societal reaction, which, through a process of identification is incorporated as part of the "me" of the individual, the probability is greatly increased that the integration of existing roles will be disrupted and that re-organization

---

44 "Primary and Secondary Deviation," in *Social Pathology: A Systematic Approach to the Theory of Sociopathic Behavior* (New York: McGrawHill, 1951).

based upon a new role or roles will occur. (The "me" in this context is simply the subjective aspect of the societal reaction.) Reorganization may be the adoption of another role in which the tendencies previously defined as "pathological" are given a more acceptable social expression. The other general possibility is the assumption of a deviant role, if such exists; or, more rarely, the person may organize an aberrant sect or group in which he creates a special role of his own. *When a person begins to employ his deviant behavior or a role based upon it as a means of defense, attack, or adjustment to the overt and covert problems created by the consequent societal reaction to him, his deviation is secondary.* Objective evidences of this change will be found in the symbolic appurtenances of the new role, in clothes, speech, posture, and mannerisms, which in some case heighten social visibility, and which in some cases serve as symbolic cues to professionalization.

Loeber, Rolf
Le Blanc, Marc
"Toward a Developmental Criminology"[45]

"Desistance" refers to the processes that lead to the cessation of crime, either entirely or in part. Contrary to activation and aggravation, which concern the building up of offending, the process of desistance concerns its decline. [...]

Le Blanc and Fréchette (1989) proposed that the process of desistance is composed of four subprocesses: *deceleration,* which refers to a reduction in frequency prior to terminating offending; *de-escalation,* the return to a less serious form of delinquency; *reaching a ceiling,* which refers to a delinquent remaining at or below a particular level of seriousness in offending without further escalating to more serious acts, and *specialization,* which refers to desistance from a versatile pattern of criminal activity to a more homogeneous pattern. It seems clear that study of the mechanism of desistance must focus exclusively on persons whose delinquency has been recurrent; one cannot speak of desistance for the occasional delinquent. Moreover, true desistance has occurred only if there is continued cessation of delinquency, rather than temporary pauses in offending.

[...]

The dearth of studies on deceleration, de-escalation, reaching a ceiling, and specialization contributes to speculation about their nature. One such speculation is that

---

45 "Toward a Developmental Criminology," *Crime and Justice* 12 (1990): 375-473.

the subprocesses probably co-occur and are intertwined in some manner. Second, each process may have distinct characteristics depending on the degree of initial aggravation in offending. [...] Third, sequences in desistance may differ depending on whether they take place during adolescence or adulthood.

The search for such differences, however, should not deny the possibility that certain general principles apply to all desistance at whatever points in the delinquent career. For example, desistance appears inversely related to progression in offending, while sequences in desistance may mirror sequences in progression. Moreover, the orthogenetic principle implies that behaviors may therefore decrease in their likelihood for desistance. In other words, we see a direct relation between the sequence of different acts that are involved in the commission of crime, progressions in their development, and their likelihood for desistance. Finally, desistance is embedded in other developmental contexts, such as a decrease in physical strength and fitness with age.

Lombroso, Cesare
Criminal Man[46]

[...] I have distinguished between the born criminal and the occasional criminal, the madman and the alcoholic, [...] and I have extended my study into primordial forms of crime among savages, children, and animals. By expanding my studies of the anatomy and physiology of criminals to include anomalies in sensitivity, in the vascular system, and in reflex reactions, I have been able to explain the paradoxical appearance of health in those who have been abnormal from birth, as are criminals. And thus I have been able to demonstrate the relationship between illness and atavism in such individuals, merging the concepts of the born criminal and the morally insane [...]

"You overly rely on isolated facts in your deductions," eminent scholars have objected to me; "if you find an asymmetrical cranium or wide-set ears in a subject, for example, you hasten to the conclusion of madness or crime; and yet, these elements have no direct or certain relation to such anomalies." —I will not respond that abnormalities are never found without reason, particularly in the case of arrested development; nor that there is a school of alienist scholars who on many occasions have not hesitated to base their diagnosis of degenerative disease on one of these anomalies. I will content myself by recalling that I do not make such deductions in theoretical isolation, but after having seen them in greater proportion among criminals than among honest men, and I will say that, in my view, an isolated anomaly is mere-

---

46 *L'Homme Criminel*, preface to the fourth edition, trans. MM. Regnier and Bournet (Paris: Félix Alcan, 1887).

ly an indication, a musical note, from which I make no presumptions nor draw any conclusions until I have discovered it in combination with other physical or mental notes. And is it nothing, in their view, to have committed a crime or to be suspected of having done so?

They will object, it is true: "How can you speak of a criminal type when your own studies show that 60 percent of them do not have such a profile?" —Aside from the fact that the figure of 40 percent is not to be discounted, the imperceptible passage from one character to another is manifested in all organic beings; it is even manifested from one species to another; this is particularly so in the field of anthropology, where individual variability, increasing in direct proportion to the advancement of civilization, appears to efface the complete criminal type.

[...]

In my view we should treat the *type* with the same caution we treat *averages* in statistics. When we say that average life expectancy is 32 years, and that the most fatal month is December, no-one understands this to mean that all men will die at the age of 32 in the month of December.

Far from jeopardizing the practical application of my conclusions, this limited way of envisaging the criminal type is favorable to it; for life imprisonment or capital punishment, the ultimate end of our research, would be impractical for a large number of men, but can be very strongly applied to a limited number. And, in regard to some individuals, we can, without apparently supporting a paradox, advise detection of this type among suspected individuals as an indication of criminality.

[...]

"You deny," objects Mr. Tarde, "the least analogy between the born criminal and the madman; and then you confound the former with the morally insane. In this way you lose sight of atavism, which has nothing to do with illness." —There is no contradiction here. The morally insane man has nothing in common with the madman; he is not ill, he is an *imbecile in the moral sense*. Furthermore, in this edition I have shown the existence, beyond those features that are truly atavistic, of acquired and entirely pathological features: facial asymmetry, for example, which is absent from the savage, strabismus, uneven ears, color blindness, unilateral paresis, uncontrollable urges, the need to hurt oneself, etc., and the sinister cheer that can be observed in their vernacular and which, alternating with a certain religiosity, is often found among epileptics. To these I add meningitis and cerebral softening, which certainly do not derive from atavism. And as a result I have come to group the morally insane and the born criminal in the epileptoid branch.

Certainly, a theory that limits itself to atavism in explaining the origin of the criminal would be much more attractive, but the truth is often less appealing than the false!

[...]

I will now respond to another accusation that I, along with Mr. Turati (*Archivio*, III), find rather singular: "This school, say a number of adversaries, was founded by men outside the science of the law, by complete intruders." But these detractors, who reproach forensic physicians for applying forensic medicine, and anthropologists for applying anthropology to social and legal questions, forget that chemists likewise apply themselves to industry, and mechanics to hydraulics and technology. They forget that Buckle and Taine first made history a serious discipline when they merged historical chronology with political economy, comparative ethnology, and psychology; finally they forget that modern physiology is nothing other than a series of applications of optics, hydraulics, etc. And how strange! While these same critics object to all attempts to reduce the danger of legislating without having studied and gained an understanding of man, solely due to their horror of an alliance with outsiders, we observe that the majority of them endure or even study not only the alliance, but the tyranny, of a science outside the law, and perhaps outside all sciences: by which I mean metaphysics. And they have had the courage to establish upon it—even on its most disputed hypotheses, such as that of free will—the laws on which social security depends!

Here I am interrupted by other jurists, who reproach me for reducing criminal law to a chapter of psychiatry, and completely overturning punishment and the prison regime! This is true only in part. In regard to occasional criminals I contain myself entirely to the sphere of common laws, and am content to ask that we further expand preventive measures. As for born criminals and the insane, the changes I propose would merely add to social security, since for them I ask permanent detention, i.e. life imprisonment in all but name.

[...]

It is said that my work seeks to destroy the Penal Code, and leave criminals in complete freedom to undermine human freedoms.

Do we not see, however, that while I diminish individual responsibility, I substitute it for that of society, which is far more demanding and severe? That while I reduce the responsibility of a group of criminals, far from seeking to soften their condition, I call for them to be permanently detained? This permanent detention is rejected by modern society in the name of theoretical principles; but in doing so it exposes itself to great danger. And moreover, are we not adopting, with infinitely more uncertainty, irregularity, and injustice, the half-continuity of punishment in the form of penal colonies, surveillance, assigned residence, etc.: incomplete measures with questionable efficacy, but by means of which society flatters itself on obtaining the security that the laws cannot provide?

[...]

It is also entirely true that, if we accept the identity of the morally insane and the born criminal, and if we recognize the existence of half-madmen, individuals possessed by systematic madness (vol. II), the able lawyer, pleading before a judge who bases sentencing on free will, will be able to paralyze the work of the justice system by revealing such a man to be ill where others saw him as guilty.

And so? Should we falsify and reject the truth so that the law, rather than accepting it, is engaged in a false path, studying the crime without studying the guilty individual? Is it not more just to amend the laws based on the facts, than to falsify the facts to accommodate the laws, simply to avoid troubling the peace of a few men who do not wish to pay attention to the new discoveries that have enriched our field of study?

[...]

Even on questions of pure law, these studies have found a broad application. Thus, the theory that substitutes the law of social defense for the religious doctrine of sin, and replaces free will with the fear of the dangers that the guilty may face, provides a solid foundation for the penal philosophy that until now had wavered ceaselessly from one side to the other without producing a result. Once and for all let us take the fear of the guilty as a criterion, and the physical and mental characteristics of the born criminal as an indication, and you will have a solution to the problem relating to the attempt, of guilty inertia followed by death, that must be punished in these miserable beings.

m

Marx, Gary T.
"The Maximal Security Society" [47]

I believe that Bentham's vision, developed almost 200 years ago, has a great deal to offer our own time. In his book, Bentham proposes a plan of the ideal prison, with the permanent inspection of prisoners and guards, and cells built with bars (rather than opaque doors) around a central surveillance tower. His ideas inspired the construction of maximum security prisons, characterized today by their perimeter security, thick walls with guard towers, spotlights, and extensive electronic surveillance.

Individuals are classified and labeled according to in-depth general examinations and predictive methods. Files play an important role. Collusive relationships between prisoners and guards and informing are the general rule. Control depends both on the physical environment (for example, furniture built into the walls) and the physiological environment (tranquillizers). Prisoners cannot move between sectors unless they are accompanied by guards and have obtained a pass. Inspection stations are frequent.

Video surveillance is omnipresent. Prisoners can be kept under surveillance in the shower and on the toilet. They are counted and frisked systematically.

47 "La société de sécurité maximale," *Déviance et Société* 12, no. 2 (1988): 147-166.

The extreme conditions of a maximum security prison can help us to understand society as a whole. Many methods of control found in prisons and criminal justice systems are now spreading into society. The techniques and "ethos" that were previously applied only to suspects or prisoners are now applied in the most benign of circumstances. It is important to ask whether the recent development of technology, culture, and social organization is pushing us to become a maximum security society.

As the prison "ethos" gradually spreads across society as a whole, the need for actual prisons may recede, as society becomes the functional alternative to prison. This has clearly long been the wish of the reform movement for correction in the community. But this movement did not foresee that the general population would in a sense become prisoners in the same way as those individuals convicted by the judicial system.

The trend in North America, and perhaps in other industrialized democracies, is to bring society closer to, rather than distance it from, maximum security. At the same time, the scientific analysis of police work (Ericson and Shearing, 1986) offers new methods and means for legitimizing the power of the police. It is both an instrument and an ideology. We find ourselves faced with a major intellectual challenge in understanding how and to what extent traditional democratic societies are at the mercy of the destruction of freedom by apparently non-violent technical means.

Marx, Karl
Theories of Surplus Value[48]

A philosopher produces ideas, a poet poems, a clergyman sermons, a professor compendia and so on. A criminal produces crimes. If we look a little closer at the connection between this latter branch of production and society as a whole, we shall rid ourselves of many prejudices. The criminal produces not only crimes but also criminal law, and with this also the professor who gives lectures on criminal law and in addition to this the inevitable compendium in which this same professor throws his lectures onto the general market as "commodities." This brings with it augmentation of national wealth, quite apart from the personal enjoyment which the [...] manuscript of the compendium brings to its originator himself.

The criminal moreover produces the whole of the police and of criminal justice, constables, judges, hangmen, juries, etc.; and all these different lines of business, which form equally many categories of the social division of labour, develop different capacities of the human spirit, create new needs and new ways of satisfying them. Torture alone has given rise to the most ingenious mechanical inventions, and employed many honourable craftsmen in the production of its instruments.

The criminal produces an impression, partly moral and partly tragic, as the case may be, and in this way renders a "service" by arousing the moral and aesthetic feelings of the public. He produces not only compendia on Crimi-

---

48 *Theories of Surplus Value,* trans. Emile Burns (Moscow: Progress Publishers, 1963).

nal Law, not only penal codes and along with them legislators in this field, but also art, belles-lettres, novels, and even tragedies, as not only Müllner's Schuld and Schiller's Räuber show, but also [Sophocles'] *Oedipus* and [Shakespeare's] *Richard the Third*. The criminal breaks the monotony and everyday security of bourgeois life. In this way he keeps it from stagnation, and gives rise to that uneasy tension and agility without which even the spur of competition would get blunted. Thus he gives a stimulus to the productive forces. While crime takes a part of the superfluous population off the labour market and thus reduces competition among the labourers—up to a certain point preventing wages from falling below the minimum—the struggle against crime absorbs another part of this population. Thus the criminal comes in as one of those natural "counterweights" which bring about a correct balance and open up a whole perspective of "useful" occupations.

The effects of the criminal on the development of productive power can be shown in detail. Would locks ever have reached their present degree of excellence had there been no thieves? Would the making of bank-notes have reached its present perfection had there been no forgers? Would the microscope have found its way into the sphere of ordinary commerce but for trading frauds? Doesn't practical chemistry owe just as much to adulteration of commodities and the efforts to show it up as to the honest zeal for production? Crime, through its constantly new methods of attack on property, constantly calls into being new methods of defence, and so is as productive as strikes for the invention of machines. And if one leaves the sphere of private crime: would the world-market ever have come into being but for national crime? Indeed, would even the nations have arisen? And hasn't the Tree of Sin been at the same time the Tree of Knowledge ever since the time of Adam? [...] "the moment, Evil ceases, the Society must be spoil'd if not totally dissolve'd."

Matza, David
Delinquency and Drift[49]

The image of the delinquent I wish to convey is one of drift; an actor neither compelled nor committed to deeds nor freely choosing them; neither different in any simple or fundamental sense from the law abiding, nor the same; conforming to certain traditions in American life while partially unreceptive to other more conventional traditions [...] .

The delinquent is casually, intermittently, and transiently immersed in a pattern of illegal action. His investment of affect in the delinquent enterprise is sufficient so as to allow an eliciting of prestige and satisfaction but not so large as to "become more or less unavailable for other lines of action." In point of fact, the delinquent is available even during the period of optimum involvement for many lines of legal and conventional action. Not only is he available but a moment's reflection tells us that, concomitant with his illegal involvement, he actively participates in a wide variety of conventional activity. If commitment implies, as it does, rendering oneself presently and in the future unavailable for other lines of action, then the delinquent is uncommitted. He is committed to neither delinquent nor conventional enterprise. Neither, by the canons of his ideology or the makeup of his personality, is precluded.

Drift stands midway between freedom and control. Its basis is an area of the social structure in which control has been loosened, coupled with the abortiveness of ad-

---

49   *Delinquency and Drift* (New York: John Wiley & Sons, Inc., 1964).

olescent endeavor to organize an autonomous subculture, and thus an independent source of control, around illegal action. The delinquent transiently exists in a limbo between convention and crime, responding in turn to the demands of each, flirting now with one, now the other, but postponing commitment, evading decision. Thus, he drifts between criminal and conventional action.

[...]

Drift is motion guided gently by underlying influences. The guidance is gentle and not constraining. The drift may be initiated or deflected by events so numerous as to defy codification. But underlying influences are operative nonetheless in that they make initiation to delinquency more probably, and they reduce the chances that an event will deflect the drifter from his delinquent path. Drift is a gradual process of movement, unperceived by the actor, in which the first stage may be accidental or unpredictable from the point of view of any theoretic frame of reference, and deflection from the delinquent path may be similarly accidental or unpredictable.

McKenzie, Roderick D.
"The Ecological Approach to the Study of Human Community" [50]

[...]

Ecology has been defined as "that phase of biology that considers plants and animals as they exist in nature, and studies their interdependence, and the relation of each kind an individual to its environment." [51]

This definition is not sufficiently comprehensive to include all the elements that logically fall within the range of human ecology. In the absence of any precedent let us tentatively define human ecology as a study of the special and temporal relations [52] of human beings as affected by the selective, distributive, and accommodative forces of the environment. Human ecology is fundamentally interested in the effect of *position* [53], in both time and space, upon human institutions and human behaviour. "Society is made up of individuals spatially separated, territorially distributed, and capable of independent locomotion." [54]

---

50 "The Ecological Approach to the Study of Human Community," *American Journal of Sociology* 30, no. 3 (November 1924): 287-301.

51 *Encyclopedia Americana* (New York: American, 1923), 555.

52 As indicated later on in this paper, ecological formations tend to develop in cyclic fashion. A period of time within which a given ecological formation develops and culminates is the time period for that particular formation. The length of these time periods may be ultimately measured and predicted, hence the inclusion of the temporal element in the definition.

53 The word "position" is used to describe the place relation of a given community to other communities, also the location of the individual or institution within the community itself.

54 Robert E. Park and Ernest W. Burgess, *Introduction to the Science of Sociology* (Chicago: University of Chicago Press, 1921), 509.

These spatial relationships of human beings are the products of competition and selection, and are continuously in process of change as new factors enter to disturb the competitive relations or to facilitate mobility. Human institutions and human nature itself become accommodated to certain spatial relationships of human beings. As these spatial relationships change, the physical basis of social relations is altered, thereby producing social and political problems.

[...]

Mendelsohn, Benjamin
"Victimology"[55]

Historically, the victim has not been adequately studied, defended by the justice system, or supported by public opinion in social life. In effect, research has not concerned itself with *the victim as a victim*. Never has the victim been considered as a concern in himself; never has he been studied as the personality of the criminal has been studied. In law the victim has always been considered—in principle—as the exclusive product of the perpetrator, which is an error. The criminal, or the harmful element, has always and in all quarters been the object of general attention, while the victim, or the suffering element, has always been left in the dark. The victim has generally been considered as *a passive factor*. The question of *if* and *when* certain weaknesses or faults in certain individuals—whether innate or acquired at a later stage—can determine *the attitude of being vulnerable* to more easily becoming a victim, has never been elevated to the level of a scientific discipline. The limited success of criminology in providing therapy and prevention for offenders has not been applied to the topic of the victim's personality. It has not been considered from this angle by biology, psychology, or sociology.

[...]

Why is society so concerned with the offender in the period of prevention, judgment, and execution of his sentence, contact with his family, his re-education (formal

---

55 "La Victimologie," *Revue Française de Psychanalyse* 22, no. 1 (1958): 95-119. Based on a paper presented to the Romanian Society of Psychiatry, March 29, 1947).

schooling, learning a trade, etc.) and his support upon release? Why does society, so human in its approach to the individual breaking the law, take no interest in the victim who, besides the suffering inflicted by the aggressor, must also endure the *onus probandi*? [...] *Why does society take an interest in the criminal? Because he is dangerous!* [...] *Why does it ignore the victim? Because he is harmless!*

[...]

Modern society has developed a science—criminology—which is also concerned with the various aspects of combating criminality, based on the personality of the offender. Is there a science that concerns itself *especially* and *specifically* with the victim? *None.* This is a strange attitude with a negative impact on science and justice, which exerts a harmful influence over everyday life. For equal treatment before the law, and for justice to be served fully and fairly, it is absolutely essential for the victim to be studied in equal measure to the criminal. The problem of criminality must also be studied in terms of the personality of the victim, from preventive and curative, biological, psychological, and sociological points of view. This new science will constitute what I shall call for the first time Victimology. It is the conception of a policy for defending society, whose principal goal will be the protective education of the members of society, in order to prevent them from becoming victims, and the therapy required to prevent them becoming repeat victims.

Merton, Robert K.
"Social Structure and Anomie"[56]

Among the elements of social and cultural structure, two are important for our purposes. These are analytically separable although they merge imperceptibly in concrete situations. The first consists of culturally defined goals, purposes, and interests. It comprises a frame of aspirational reference. These goals are more or less integrated and involve varying degrees of prestige and sentiment. They constitute a basic, but not the exclusive, component of what Linton aptly has called "designs for group living." Some of these cultural aspirations are related to the original drives of man, but they are not determined by them. The second phase of the social structure defines, regulates, and controls the acceptable modes of achieving these goals. Every social group invariably couples its scale of desired ends with moral or institutional regulation of permissible and required procedures for attaining these ends. These regulatory norms and moral imperatives do not necessarily coincide with technical or efficiency norms. Many procedures which from the standpoint of particular individuals would be most efficient in securing desired values, e.g., illicit oil-stock schemes, theft, fraud, are ruled out of the institutional area of permitted conduct. The choice of expedients is limited by the institutional norms.

To say that these two elements, culture goals and institutional norms, operate jointly is not to say that the ranges of alternative behaviours and aims bear some constant

---

56 "Social Structure and Anomie," *American Sociological Review* 3, no. 5 (October 1938): 672682.

relation to one another. The emphasis upon certain goals may vary independently of the degree of emphasis upon institutional means. There may develop a disproportionate, at times, a virtually exclusive, stress upon the value of specific goals, involving relatively slight concern with the institutionally appropriate modes of attaining these goals. The limiting case in this direction is reached when the range of alternative procedures is limited only by technical rather than institutional considerations. Any and all devices which promise attainment of the all important goal would be permitted in this hypothetical polar case.

This constitutes one type of cultural malintegration. A second polar type is found in groups where activities originally conceived as instrumental are transmuted into ends in themselves. The original purposes are forgotten and ritualistic adherence to institutionally prescribed conduct becomes virtually obsessive. Stability is largely ensured while change is flouted. The range of alternative behaviours is severely limited. There develops a tradition-bound, sacred society characterized by neophobia. The occupational psychosis of the bureaucrat may be cited as a case in point. Finally, there are the intermediate types of groups where a balance between culture goals and institutional means is maintained. These are the significantly integrated and relatively stable, though changing, groups.

[...]

Of the types of groups which result from the independent variation of the two phases of the social structure, we shall be primarily concerned with the first, namely, that involving a disproportionate accent on goals. This statement must be recast in a proper perspective. In no group is there an absence of regulatory codes governing conduct, yet groups do vary in the degree to which these folkways, mores, and institutional controls are effectively integrated with the more diffuse goals which are part of the culture matrix. Emotional convictions may cluster about the complex of socially acclaimed ends, meanwhile shifting their support from the culturally defined implementation of these ends. As we shall see, certain aspects of the social structure may generate counter-mores and antisocial behaviour precisely because of differential emphases on goals and regulations. In the extreme case, the latter may be so vitiated by the goal-emphasis that the range of behaviour is limited only by considerations of technical expediency. The sole significant question then becomes, which available means is most efficient in netting the socially approved value? The technically most feasible procedure, whether legitimate or not, is preferred to the institutionally prescribed conduct. As this process continues, the integration of the society becomes tenuous and anomie ensues.

[...]

The process whereby exaltation of the end generates a literal demoralization, i.e., a deinstitutionalization, of the means is one which characterizes many groups in which the two phases of the social structure are not highly integrated. The extreme emphasis upon the accumulation of wealth as a symbol of success in our own society militates against the completely effective control of institutionally regulated modes of acquiring a fortune.

Fraud, corruption, vice, crime, in short, the entire catalogue of proscribed behaviour, becomes increasingly common when the emphasis on the culturally induced success-goal becomes divorced from a coordinated institutional emphasis.

Mucchielli, Roger
How They Become Offenders [57]

Since the ordinary criminal is not ill, we should stop posing the problem of delinquency in terms of psychopathology or even in terms of psychology as such. It should be situated in its true plane: the moral plane. [...] I argue that cases of true delinquency do not result from an alteration of self-control but an alteration of sociomoral conscience.

[...]

What then is this moral conscience? What is the nature of its alteration and how does it occur? These are the questions that must be answered.

It is not a philosophical problem, as our permanent reference will be the phenomenon of Delinquency. The moral conscience in question will be viewed uniquely as a dynamic factor of integration and social participation, as a Social-Desire. The amorality that concerns us is dissociality [...] The alteration will therefore be defined uniquely in terms of *social bonds*. A sociopathology is therefore required in order to explain delinquency: a specific chapter in the vast field of pathology, entirely distinct from psychopathology, psychiatry, and sociatry (this latter science focusing on pathological forms of social structures or illnesses of social groups as such). Sociopathology will be the study of alterations in human socio-moral conscience, and, primarily, the mechanisms generating the offending structure as a type of dissociality.

---

57   *Comment Ils Deviennent Délinquants* (Paris: Éditions ESF, 1974).

The true offender is *normal* from a physiological and psychological point of view. He is *abnormal* from a psychosocial point of view, and is so not in relation to the laws of his time [...] but in relation to society as such, the social dimension essential to human beings.

[...]

Of course, the normal human personality involves, if not requires, socialization; if it is successful and complete, it achieves authentic morality. But the personality can develop in a certain way *outside socialization*. Development nevertheless occurs, culminating in a chronicity that is perfectly viable in itself but will be an anomaly of varying degrees of monstrosity. A certain social bond is constructed, but in a sociopathological mode. It is the mechanisms and stages of this complex process that must be analyzed.

n

Newman, Oscar
Defensible Space: Crime Prevention Through Urban Design[58]

Defensible space is a model for residential environments which inhibits crime by creating the physical expression of a social fabric that defends itself. All the different elements which combine to make a defensible space have a common goal—an environment in which latent territoriality and sense of community in the inhabitants can be translated into responsibility for ensuring a safe, productive, and well-maintained living space. The potential criminal perceives such a space as controlled by its residents, leaving him an intruder easily recognized and dealt with.

[...]

"Defensible space" is a surrogate term for the range of mechanisms—real and symbolic barriers, strongly defined areas of influence, and improved opportunities for surveillance—that combine to bring an environment under the control of its residents. A defensible space is a living residential environment which can be employed by inhabitants for the enhancement of their lives, while providing security for their families, neighbors and friends.

[...]

---

58   *Defensible Space: Crime Prevention Through Urban Design* (New York: Macmillan, 1972).

In the evolution of human habitat over the past thousands of years, men in every culture have developed cogent devices to define the territorial realm of their dwellings. The nature and function of these mechanisms evolved slowly through change and adaptation during use. So long as human environment was built within a tradition, simply repeating previous forms ensured the preservation of past learned experience. With the breakdown of building tradition, through the rapid evolution of new techniques and the need to answer the pressing problem of accommodating higher densities, the simple repetition of past practice has become difficult, if not impossible. Unfortunately, the accumulated traditions inherent in the residential forms of the past were not held within the conscious verbal bank of human knowledge. In architectural history there is ample evidence of territorial definition and symbolization in the forms of previous residential environments. There is unfortunately no parallel evidence of their overt discussion. The tradition, grown over thousands of years in man's piecemeal search for a form of residence in an urban setting, has been lost.

In building the residential environments of twentieth-century cities, there was no reference to tradition, simply because the needs seemed so totally new and unlike any experience in the past. In our rush to provide housing for the urban immigrants and to accommodate our high population growth rates, we have been building *more* without really asking *what?*

[...]

Defensible space design returns to the productive use of residents the public areas beyond the doors of individual apartments: the hallways, lobbies, grounds, and surrounding streets—areas which are now beyond the control of inhabitants. Four elements of physical design, acting both individually and in concert, contribute to the creation of secure environments.

- The territorial definition of space in developments reflecting the areas of influence of the inhabitants. This works by subdividing the residential environment into zones toward which adjacent residents easily adopt proprietary attitudes.

- The positioning of apartment windows to allow residents to naturally survey the exterior and interior public areas of their living environment.

- The adoption of building forms which avoid the stigma of peculiarity that allow others to perceive the vulnerability and isolation of the inhabitants.

- The enhancement of safety by locating residential developments in functionally sympathetic urban areas immediately adjacent to activities that do not provide continued threat.

P

Park, Robert Ezra
"The Urban Community" [59]

[...]

Human ecology, as sociologists conceive it, seeks to emphasize not so much geography as space. In society we not only live together, but at the same time we live apart, and human relations can always be reckoned, with more or less accuracy, in terms of distance. In so far as social structure can be defined in terms of position, social changes may be described in terms of movement; and society exhibits, in one of its aspects, characters that can be measured and described in mathematical formulas.

[...]

One of the incidents of the growth of the community is the social selection and segregation of the population, and the creation, on the one hand, of natural social groups, and on the other, of natural social areas. We have become aware of this process of segregation in the case of the immigrants, and particularly in the case of the so-called historical races, peoples who, whether immigrants or not, are distinguished by racial marks. The Chinatowns, the Little Sicilies, and the other so-called "ghettos" with which students of urban life are familiar

---

59   Originally published as "The Concept of Position in Sociology," *Publications of the American Sociological Society* 20 (1925): 1-14.

are special types of a more general species of natural area which the conditions and tendencies of city life inevitably produce.

Such segregations of population as these take place, first, upon the basis of language and of culture, and second, upon the basis of race. Within these immigrant colonies and racial ghettos, however, other processes of selection inevitably take place which bring about segregation based upon vocational interests, upon intelligence, and personal ambition. The result is that the keener, the more energetic, and the more ambitious very soon emerge from their ghettos and immigrant colonies and move into an area of second immigrant settlement, or perhaps into a cosmopolitan area in which the members of several immigrant and racial groups meet and live side by side. More and more, as the ties of race, of language, and of culture are weakened, successful individuals move out and eventually find their places in business and in the professions, among the older population group which has ceased to be identified with any language or racial group. The point is that change of occupation, personal success or failure—changes of economic and social status, in short—tend to be registered in changes of location. The physical or ecological organization of the community, in the long run, responds to and reflects the occupational and the cultural.

Social selection and segregation, which create the natural groups, determine at the same time the natural areas of the city.

Pinatel, Jean

"Criminality Today"[60]

Today, as in the past, the subject of criminology is the genesis and dynamics of crime. It follows that criminological theory must provide a definition of crime conducive to an approach that opens up wide perspectives for research, carried out based on a rigorous methodology.

[...]

The principle of the approach to the genesis and dynamics of crime can be outlined based on a geometric allegory, inspired by the work of Mendes Correa. Let us imagine a cone and place the criminal act on its summit. Biological and social factors (the personal environment) occupy the base circumference, the edge of the base; the offender's personality is at the center of the base; and the criminal situation in which the offender finds himself is placed in the axis of the cone. Generating lines may directly link biological factors and personal environment factors to the offending act, but in the majority of cases, such factors have merely an indirect influence on the crime through the intermediary of the personality and the situation. I should add that this cone is immersed in general society, which emits stimuli that may have an inhibiting or encouraging effect on biological factors and the personal environment.

The result of this geometric allegory is that the offender's personality is at the center of the approach to the dynamics of crime.

---

60 "La criminalité d'aujourd'hui," *Déviance et Société* 1, no. 1 (1977): 87-93.

The instrument enabling development of this approach is the model of criminal personality. I must emphasize, to avoid all misunderstanding, that this model does not reflect an anthropological and fixist view, such as the Lombrosian criminal type. Firstly, it posits that there is no natural difference between offenders and non-offenders. There are only differences of degree or structure between them, which also enable differentiation of offenders between themselves. Secondly, it states that the personality is dynamic, never fixed but ever-evolving.

The model of criminal personality has been developed from a broad exploration of the criminology literature. From such exploration I have discovered:

1. that certain personality traits are found in all studies: egocentrism, lability, affective indifference, and aggression.

2. that other personality traits are not of the same universal nature: these are traits of temperament (some offenders are active, others passive), aptitude (physical, intellectual, and socioprofessional abilities that vary among subjects), and needs (nutritional and sexual needs, which are also affected by a strong coefficient of variability).

These results are facts. They are verifiable.

These facts have been enhanced by an interpretation with heuristic objectives. I in effect posed the principle:

1. that egocentrism, lability, affective indifference, and aggression constitute the central core of the

criminal personality, which determines entry into criminality.

2. that the other traits constitute variants or variables of the criminal personality and influence only the methods by which the individual enters criminality, his direction, success, and motivations.

In doing so, I have provided criminological research with a specific model that enables both study of entry into criminality and an approach to general society. Firstly, it reveals the action and interaction of personality traits in the path that leads to the criminal act. Secondly, it identifies the elements of general society that might encourage and stimulate the interplay of such traits at an individual level.

In other words, the model of criminal personality is situated on the cusp of the clinical and the sociological. Clinically, it opens up increasingly fine perspectives for analysis. Sociologically, it enables overall determinisms to be taken into consideration. In such circumstances I need not outline its heuristic significance.

Pinel, Philippe
Medico-Philosophical Treatise on Mental Alienation[61]

The sustained use of chains is an admirable invention for perpetuating the fury of maniacal patients with their state of detention, for making up for the lack of enthusiasm of an unenlightened superintendent, for maintaining constant exasperation and a focused desire to get revenge in the patients' hearts, and for stirring up racket and commotion in hospices. These drawbacks had been an object of concern for me whilst carrying out my responsibilities as physician at Bicêtre during the first years of the Revolution, and it was not without great regret that I could see no happy end to this barbaric and routine-minded custom. However, on the other hand I remained calm and relied on the skill of the superintendent of this hospice (M. Pussin), who was equally keen to end this neglect of true principles. Fortunately this happened two years later (4th Prairial Year VI) and there was never any development better devised, nor followed by more outstanding success. Forty wretched patients who groaned under the weight of the irons for varying numbers of years were set free in spite of all the apprehensions registered by the Central Bureau, and they were allowed to wander about freely in the courtyards simply with the movements of their arms restricted by a strait-jacket. At night they were loose in their lodge.

[...]

---

61   *Medico-Philosophical Treatise on Mental Alienation. Second Edition, Entirely Reworked and Extensively Expanded* [1809], trans. Gordon Hickish, David Healy, and Louis C. Charland (Chippenham: Wiley-Blackwell, 2008).

The insane, far from being culprits who need punishment, are patients whose sad state deserves all the consideration due to suffering humanity and whose lapsed reason one must seek to restore by the simplest means.

q

Quetelet, Adolphe
"On Moral Statistics and the Principles That Should Form its Basis"[62]

Moral facts essentially differ from physical facts by the involvement of a specific cause that at first sight appears to evade all our expectations, i.e. the involvement of man's free will.

However, experience teaches us that free will exerts its action only in a limited sphere, and that, while highly apparent to individuals, it has no discernible effect on the social body, where all individual particularities are in some way neutralized.

When we consider man generally, moral and physical facts are influenced by the same causes and must be submitted to the same principles of observation. Yet the causes that influence our social system generally only suffer slow, one might say secular, changes; hence, the remarkable permanency that dominates social factors such as marriage, crime, suicide, etc.

In moral statistics, elements cannot be measured in a direct manner; it becomes necessary to rely on the principle that effects are proportional to the causes that produce them.

---

62   "Sur la statistique morale et les principes qui doivent en former la base," *Mémoires de l'Académie Royale des Sciences, des Lettres et des Beaux-Arts de Belgique* 21 (1848): 1-68.

When we observe the same class of facts, their degree of frequency allows us to judge the degree of tendency to produce them. Tendency determined in this manner is in no way absolute; there is no unit that can serve as a measure, and it can have only a relative value, i.e. a value comparative to other tendencies of the same nature. Thus, supposing that a million men aged 35 to 40 marry twice as often as a million men aged 45 to 50, we can say that the tendency to marriage in the first group is double that of the second group.

Tendency deduced from the observation of facts is only apparent, etc. in certain circumstances, and may vary considerably from the true tendency. This is the case for poisonings, for example; since, despite the activities of the law, a large number of these crimes still remain unknown.

In many cases we can substitute apparent tendencies for true tendencies. Thus, according to documents in France, all other things being equal, we count twice as many poisonings in the group aged 45 to 50 as in the group aged 55 to 60. The tendency to poisoning, for the first group, is thus double than it is for the second; and arguably this apparent tendency is in line with the true tendency, if the justice system is equally active in identifying guilty parties aged 45 to 50 as those aged 55 to 60. In this case, the numbers compared are, in truth, lower than the real numbers, but they are found to be lower in the same ratio.

Only homogeneous facts can be compared; thus, general reports on criminal justice in France are not comparable to the general reports that England annually publishes on the actions of its courts, and even when we draw comparisons within France, this can only be for crimes of the same nature.

By limiting ourselves to one order of facts gathered in one country, it also happens that these facts do not all have the same importance; there is an infinity of nuances among them. However, when we study a large number of men, we consider their moral qualities as well as their physical qualities: we can suppose an average term around which all the elements observed cluster, some more than others. In addition, they arrange themselves according to a determined law, which is the law of possibility and which is the same for all the facts subject to the influence of accidental causes.

These are, ultimately, the averages that are compared, and these averages are even more distinct from all the accidental causes, because the observations are spread across a large number of men.

These principles have been applied to the formation of a table of criminality: a table that indicates the degree of tendency toward crime in different ages. And this law of development in tending toward crime has turned out to be the same in France, Belgium, the Grand Duchy of Baden, and in England, the only countries for which the data is widely available.

This law has been perfectly consistent, according to the individual results from each year, for the nineteen years that France has published its court documents.

The tendency to crime increases very rapidly toward adulthood; it reaches a peak and then declines toward the very end of life. This law appears to be constant and varies only in its scale and the peak period.

In France, for general crimes, the peak is around 24 years; in Belgium, this critical period arrives two years later; while in England and in the Grand Duchy of Baden, it is observed earlier.

There is a difference between the sexes: in France, the peak for men occurs around one year earlier than in women, and is four times higher.

There is also a difference in the nature of crimes: thus, for crimes against property, the peak occurs around two years earlier than the tendency to crime against persons, and is two to three times greater. If we consider the main classes of crime separately, they may be placed in the following order by precocity: theft, rape, assault and battery, murder, premeditated murder, poisoning, and fraud of all kinds.

r

Radzinowicz, Léon
In Search of Criminology[63]

Every country faces the problems of crime and of punishment, which are the stuff of criminology. Yet it is only too evident that the scope of criminology as an academic discipline is still somewhat blurred and confused. What, after all, is criminology about? How should it be explored and how should it be taught? What is it for?

Too much time is still being spent, especially on the continent of Europe, in trying to construct an elaborate and exhaustive definition of criminology, in dividing and subdividing its various departments of interest, and in assigning to each of them a different title, while at the same time insisting that these various pursuits are interconnected and cannot be followed in isolation from each other. [...]

Some twenty different terms are in use, and they make a bewildering list: criminology; criminal science; criminal anthropology; criminal biology; criminal psychology; criminal (or forensic) psychiatry; judicial psychology; criminal sociology; penal philosophy; penal policy; criminal policy; criminal jurisprudence; criminal statistics; penology; prison science; prison law; prison pedagogy; police science; criminalistics; criminal prophylaxis. Though these varied titles represent the several emerging lines of a new discipline, it is difficult to justify such a

---

63 *In Search of Criminology* (London: Heinemann, 1961).

wealth of expressions, and the confusion is increased by the fact that many of them have different meanings for different authors.

I do not deny the need to consider the content of criminology, but I deprecate those elaborate subdivisions and the rather naïve belief that clear-cut definitions can be achieved and can serve a useful purpose in advancing criminological knowledge. [...]

It is not a definition that is needed but a workmanlike description of functions. Criminology, in its narrow sense, is concerned with the study of the phenomenon of crime and of the factors or circumstances—individual and environmental—which may have an influence on, or be associated with, criminal behaviour and the state of crime in general. But this does not, and should not, exhaust the whole subject matter of criminology. There remains the vitally important problem of combating crime. The systematic study of all the measures to be taken in the spheres of prevention (direct and indirect), of legislation, of the enforcement of the criminal law, of punishments and other methods of treatment, constitutes an indisputable and integral part of criminology. To rob it of this practical function is to divorce criminology from reality and render it sterile.

Reiss, Rodolphe Archibald
"Scientific Methods in Criminal Investigations"[64]

[...] it must be acknowledged that criminality is developing, and its methods of action are being refined in line with scientific progress.

It is the magistrates and police who are tasked with defending the honest part of the population from the criminal or untouchable part. But it also falls upon them to find the perpetrator of the crime once it has been committed, and finally to thwart the machinations of wrongdoers in order to prevent new crimes. This identification of the criminal and any accomplices he may have is becoming increasingly difficult due to the ease of communications enabling individuals to travel a long distance in a very short space of time, and also due to the increasing refinement with which crimes (particularly crimes against property) are committed.

The old police methods of the last fifty years are no longer sufficient today; criminals must be fought with weapons of equal if not greater finesse, and this is possible only through the introduction of scientific methods into criminal investigations. The application of scientific methods to criminal investigations is fairly new. It is due to the efforts of eminent criminologists and scientists such as Bertillon, Gross, the Minovici brothers, Lacassagne, Galton, Henry, etc., and has led to the creation of a special scientific branch known as the "Forensic Police."

---

64   "Les méthodes scientifiques dans les enquêtes judiciaires et policières," *Archives d'Anthropologie Criminelle, de Criminologie et de Psychologie Normale et Pathologique* 21 (1906): 857-876.

Rusche, Georg
"Labor Market and Penal Sanction"[65]

It can be said without contradiction that crimes are acts which are forbidden in society. Debates about the meaning of punishment will not be addressed here. I shall not discuss whether the goal of punishment is retribution, deterrence, or reform of the criminal. One thing, though is certain: no society wants its penal system to incite the commission of crimes. In other words, punishment has to be constituted in such a way that those people who appear to be criminally inclined or inclined to commit acts that are undesirable to the society, are at least not encouraged to do so by the prospect of being discovered and punished. On the contrary, it is even hoped that the prospect of punishment will deter if not all members of this class, then at least a substantial part.

Indeed, the anticipation of future suffering and painful reprisal, which by far exceed the possible pleasurable gain, should be an effective counterbalance for any rational person. Now experience teaches us that most crimes are committed by members of those strata who are burdened by strong social pressures and who are relatively disadvantaged in satisfying their needs when compared to other classes. Therefore, a penal sanction, if it is not to be counter-productive, must be constituted in such a way that the classes which are most criminally inclined prefer to abstain from the forbidden acts than become victims of criminal punishment.

---

65 "Labor Market and Penal Sanction: Thoughts on the Sociology of Criminal Justice [1933]," trans. Gerda Dinwiddie, in Why Punish? How Much?: A Reader on Punishment, edited by Michael H. Tonry (Oxford: Oxford University Press, 2011), 405-413.

[...]

Criminality certainly occurs throughout all social classes. But [...] it becomes clear that the criminal law and
the daily work of the criminal courts are directed almost exclusively against those people whose class background, poverty, neglected education, or demoralization
drove them to crime.

[...]

If penal sanctions are supposed to deter these strata from
crime in an effective manner, they must appear even worse
than the strata's present living conditions. One can also
formulate this proposition as follows: all efforts to reform
the punishment of criminals are inevitably limited by the
situation of the lowest socially significant proletarian class
that society wants to deter from criminal acts. All reform
efforts, however humanitarian and well meaning, which
attempt to go beyond this restriction are condemned to
utopianism. If penal reforms should be demanded by
public opinion and carried out, the reforms would have to
be undermined by a more subtle deterioration of prison
conditions. For a genuine improvement in the conditions
of imprisonment beyond this limit would no longer deter
such large groups of people, and, as a consequence, the
purpose of punishment would be destroyed.

[...]

The history of the penal system is more than a history
of the alleged independent development of legal "institutions." It is the history of the relations of the "two nations," as Disraeli called them, that constitute a people—
the rich and the poor.

S

Shaw, Clifford R.
McKay, Henry D.
Juvenile Delinquency and Urban Areas[66]

It is clear from the data included in this volume that there is a direct relationship between conditions existing in local communities of American cities and differential rates of delinquents and criminals. Communities with high rates have social and economic characteristics which differentiate them from communities with low rates. Delinquency—particularly group delinquency, which constitutes a preponderance of all officially recorded offences committed by boys and young men—has its roots in the dynamic life of the community.

It is recognized that the data included in this volume may be interpreted from many different points of view. However, the high degree of consistency in the association between delinquency and other characteristics of the community not only sustains the conclusion that delinquent behavior is related dynamically to the community but also appears to establish that all community characteristics, including delinquency, are products of the operation of general processes more or less common to American cities. Moreover, the fact that in Chicago the rates of delinquents for many years have remained relatively constant in the areas adjacent to centers of commerce and heavy industry, despite successive changes in the nativity

---

66 *Juvenile Delinquency and Urban Areas* (Chicago: The University of Chicago Press, 1942).

and nationality composition of the population, supports emphatically the conclusion that the delinquency-producing factors are inherent in the community.

From the data available, it appears that local variations in the conduct of children, as revealed in the differential rates of delinquents, reflect the differences in social values, norms, and attitudes to which the children are exposed. In some parts of the city, attitudes which support and sanction delinquency are, it seems, sufficiently extensive and dynamic to become the controlling forces in the development of delinquent careers among a relatively large number of boys and young men. These are the low-income areas, where delinquency has developed in the form of a social tradition, inseparable from the life of the local community.

Sherman, Lawrence W.
"Defiance, Deterrence and Irrelevance:
A Theory of the Criminal Sanction" [67]

Defiance is the net increase in the prevalence, incidence, or seriousness of future offending against a sanctioning community caused by a proud, shameless reaction to the administration of a criminal sanction. Specific or individual defiance is the reaction of one person to that person's own punishment. General defiance is the reaction of a group or collectivity to the punishment of one or more of its members. Direct defiance is a crime committed against a sanctioning agent. Indirect defiance is the displaced just deserts committed against a target vicariously representing the sanctioning agents provoking the anger. Defiance is distinct from other hypothetical mechanisms by which sanctions increase crime, such as labeling (Lemert 1972), thrill seeking (Katz 1988), imitation, or brutalization (Bowers 1988). Defiance theory explains variation in criminal events, not criminality. Defiance theory may encompass many types of crimes but may also be more powerful a predictor of predatory and competitive offenses than of mutualistic or retreatist offenses (Felson 1987).

[...]

Defiance occurs under four conditions, all of which are necessary.

    1.   The offender defines a criminal sanction as unfair.

---

67 "Defiance, Deterrence and Irrelevance: A Theory of the Criminal Sanction," *Journal of Research in Crime and Delinquency* 30, no. 4 (November 1993): 445-473.

2. The offender is poorly bonded to or alienated from the sanctioning agent or the community the agent represents.

3. The offender defines the sanction as stigmatizing and rejecting a person, not a lawbreaking act.

4. The offender denies or refuses to acknowledge the shame the sanction has actually caused him to suffer.

Sanctions are defined as unfair under two conditions, either of which is sufficient:

1. The sanctioning agent behaves with disrespect for the offender, or for the group to which the offender belongs, regardless of how fair the sanction is on substantive grounds.

2. The sanction is substantively arbitrary, discriminatory, excessive, undeserved, or otherwise objectively unjust.

Offenders deny shame as one of the two adaptive responses to alienation, as Karl Marx put it: "impotence and indignation" (quoted in Scheff and Retzinger 191, p. 64). The first response accepts shame and seeks escape through retreat or intoxicants, as in Anderson's (1978) "wineheads." The second denies shame and insulates against it by anger and rage in reaction to insult, as in Anderson's "hoodlums." We lack sufficient evidence or theory to specify the individual or social conditions under which alienated persons choose these alternative responses.

Defiance theory therefore predicts three reactions to punishment defined as unfair.

1. When poorly bonded offenders accept the shame an unfair stigmatizing sanction provokes, the sanction will be *irrelevant* or possibly even deterrent to future rates of offending.

2. When poorly bonded offenders deny the shame they feel and respond with rage, the unfair stigmatizing sanction will *increase* their future rates of offending. This unacknowledged shame leads to an emotion of angry pride at defying the punishment. That pride predisposes the defiant offender to repeat the sanctioned conduct, symbolically labeling the sanctions or sanctioners, and not the offender's own acts, as truly shameful and morally deserving of punishment. In the process, the victims or targets of the sanctioned acts become vicarious substitutes for the state or its sanctioning representatives.

3. The full shame-crime sequence does not occur, however, when a well-bonded offender defines a sanction as unfair. The unfairness may weaken the deterrent effect of the sanction and make it irrelevant to future conduct. But even if the offender [...] denies the shame, proud defiance is unlikely because it is less valued than the pride associated with social bonds.

Sherman, Lawrence W.
"Hot Spots of Crime and Criminal Careers of Places"[68]

[...]

Hot spots, as defined here, are *small places in which the occurrence of crime is so frequent that it is highly predictable, at least over a one year period.* Within this definition, the phenomenon of hot spots appears to be widespread in the U.S. and elsewhere.

In Minneapolis, for example, an analysis of 323,000 calls to the police in 1986 found that a small number of hot spots produced most of the crime in the city (Sherman et al., 1989). Only 3% of the places produced 50% of the calls to which the police were dispatched. This concentration was even greater for the predatory crimes of robbery, criminal sexual conduct and auto theft: only 5% of the 115,000 street addresses and intersections in the city produced 100% of the calls for those, usually stranger-perpetrated, offenses.

[...]

The concentration of crime in a few hot places seems even greater when it is compared to the concentration of crime among individuals (Spelman and Eck, 1989). Wolfgang and his colleagues' (1972) examination of a 1945 Philadelphia cohort found that 18% of the individuals produced over 50% of the arrests, compared to the

---

68   "Hot Spots of Crime and Criminal Careers of Places," in *Crime and Place: Crime Prevention Studies*, vol. 1, edited by John E. Eck and David Weisburd (Monsey, New York: Criminal Justice Press, 1995), 35-52.

3% of places producing 50% of calls in Minneapolis. If we disregard the differences between the cities and the possible effect of 17 more years of observation in Philadelphia than Minneapolis, it is striking that the concentration of crime among places is six times greater than it is among persons.

This comparison raises profound questions for both criminological theory and crime control policy. For if future crime is six times more predictable by the address of the occurrence than by the identity of the offender, why aren't we doing more about it? Why aren't we thinking more about wheredunit, rather than just whodunit?

Sutherland, Edwin
"The Problem of White Collar Crime" [69]

The thesis of this book, stated positively, is that persons of the upper socio-economic class engage in much criminal behaviour.

[...]

These violations of law by persons in the upper socio-economic class are, for convenience, called "white-collar crimes." This concept is not intended to be definitive, but merely to call attention to crimes which are not ordinarily included within the scope of criminology. White-collar crime may be defined approximately as a crime committed by a person of respectability and high social status in the course of his occupation. Consequently, it excludes many crimes of the upper class, such as most of their cases of murder, adultery, and intoxication, since these are not customarily a part of their occupational procedures. Also, it excludes the confidence games of wealthy members of the under-world, since they are not persons of respectability and high social status.

The significant thing about white-collar crime is that it is not associated with poverty or with social and personal pathologies which accompany poverty. If it can be shown that white-collar crimes are frequent, a general theory that crime is due to poverty and its related pathologies is shown to be invalid. Furthermore, the study of white-collar crime may assist in locating those factors which, being common to the crimes of the rich and the

---

69 "The Problem of White Collar Crime," in *White Collar Crime* (New York: The Dryden Press, 1949).

poor, are most significant for a general theory of criminal behavior.

Sutherland, Edwin
Principles of Criminology [70]

The following statements refer to the process by which a particular person comes to engage in criminal behavior:

1. *Criminal behavior is learned.* Negatively, this means that criminal behavior is not inherited, as such. Also, the person who has not been trained in crime does not invent criminal behavior, just as the person who has had no training in mechanics does not make mechanical inventions.

2. *Criminal behavior is learned in interaction with other persons in a process of communication.* This communication is verbal in many respects, but it also includes "the communication of gestures."

3. *The principal part of the learning of criminal behavior occurs within intimate personal groups.* Negatively, this means that the impersonal agencies of communication, such as movies and newspapers, play a relatively unimportant part in the genesis of criminal behavior.

4. *When criminal behavior is learned, the learning includes (a) techniques of committing the crime, which are sometimes very complicated, sometimes very simple; (b) the specific direction of motives, drives, rationalizations, and attitudes.*

5. *The specific direction of motives and drives is learned from definitions of the legal codes as favorable or*

70 *Principles of Criminology* (Chicago: J. B. Lippincott Co, 4th edition, 1947).

unfavorable. In some societies the individual is surrounded by persons who invariably define the legal codes as rules to be observed, while in others the individual is surrounded by persons whose definitions are almost always mixed, with the consequence that there is normative conflict in relation to the legal codes. In American society these definitions are almost always mixed, with the consequence that there is normative conflict in relation to the legal codes.

6. *A person becomes delinquent because of an excess of definitions favorable to violation of law over definitions unfavorable to violation of law.* This is the principle of differential association. It refers to both criminal and anticriminal associations and involves counteracting forces. When persons become criminal, they do so because of contacts with criminal behavior patterns and also because of isolation from anticriminal behavior patterns. Any person inevitably assimilates the surrounding culture unless other patterns are in conflict. Thus a southerner does not pronounce *r* because other southerners do not pronounce *r*. Negatively, this proposition of differential association means that associations which are neutral—as far as crime is concerned—have little or no effect on the genesis of criminal behavior. Much of the experience of a person is neutral in this sense, such as learning to brush one's teeth. This behavior has no positive or negative effect on criminal behavior except as it may be related to associations which are concerned with the

legal codes. Such neutral behavior is important especially in occupying the time of a child so that he or she is not in contact with criminal behavior while engaged in the neutral behavior.

7. *Differential associations may vary in frequency, duration, priority, and intensity.* This means that associations with criminal behavior and associations with anticriminal behavior vary in those respects. Frequency and duration as modalities of associations are obvious and need no explanation. Priority is assumed to be important in the sense that lawful behavior developed in early childhood may persist throughout life, and also that delinquent behavior developed in early childhood may persist throughout life. This tendency, however, has not been adequately demonstrated, and priority seems to be important principally through its selective influence. Intensity is not precisely defined, but it has to do with such things as the prestige of the source of a criminal or anticriminal pattern and with emotional reactions related to the associations. In a precise description of the criminal behavior of a person, these modalities would be rated in quantitative form and a mathematical ratio would be reached. A formula in this sense has not been developed, and the development of such a formula would be extremely difficult.

8. *The process of learning criminal behavior by association with criminal and anticriminal patterns involves all of the mechanisms that are involved in any other learning.* Negatively, this means that

the learning of criminal behavior is not restricted to the process of imitation. A person who is
seduced, for instance, learns criminal behavior
by association, but this process would not ordinarily be described as imitation.

9. *While criminal behavior is an expression of general
needs and values, it is not explained by those general needs and values.* Thieves generally steal in order to secure money, but likewise honest labor-
ers work in order to secure money. The attempts
by many scholars to explain criminal behavior
by general drives and values, such as the happiness principle, striving for social status, the
money motive, or frustration, have been, and
continue to be, futile, since they explain lawful
behavior as completely as they explain criminal
behavior. Such drives and values are similar to
respiration, which is necessary for any behavior
but does not differentiate criminal from non-
criminal behavior.

Sykes, Gresham
Matza, David
"Techniques of Neutralization"[71]

In attempting to uncover the roots of juvenile delinquency, the social scientist has long since ceased to search for devils in the mind or stigma of the body. It is now largely agreed that delinquent behavior, like most social behavior, is learned and that it is learned in the process of social interaction.

The classic statement of this position is found in Sutherland's theory of differential association, which asserts that criminal or delinquent behavior involves the learning of (a) techniques of committing crimes and (b) motives, drives, rationalizations, and attitudes favorable to the violation of law. Unfortunately, the specific content of what is learned—as opposed to the process by which it is learned—has received relatively little attention in either theory or research. Perhaps the single strongest school of thought on the nature of this content has centered on the idea of a delinquent subculture. The basic characteristic of the delinquent subculture, it is argued, is a system of values that represents and inversion of the values help by respectable, law-abiding society. The world of the delinquent is the world of the law-abiding turned upside down and its norms constitute a countervailing force directed against the conforming social order. Cohen sees the process of developing a delinquent subculture as a matter of building, maintaining, and reinforcing a code for behavior which exists by opposition, which stands in

71 "Techniques of Neutralization: A Theory of Delinquency," *American Sociological Review* 22, no. 6 (December 1957): 664670.

point by point contradiction to dominant values, particularly those of the middle class.

[...]

It is our argument that much delinquency is based on what is essentially an unrecognized extension of defenses to crimes, in the form of justifications for deviance that are seen as valid by the delinquent but not by the legal system or society at large.

These justifications are commonly described as rationalizations. They are viewed as following deviant behavior and as protecting the individual from self-blame and the blame of others after the act. But there is also reason to believe that they precede deviant behavior and make deviant behavior possible. It is this possibility that Sutherland mentioned only in passing and that other writers have failed to exploit from the viewpoint of sociological theory. Disapproval flowing from internalized norms and conforming others in the social environment is neutralized, turned back, or deflected in advance. Social controls that serve to check or inhibit deviant motivational patterns are rendered inoperative, and the individual is freed to engage in delinquency without serious damage to his self image. In this sense, the delinquent both has his cake and eats it too, for he remains committed to the dominant normative system and yet so qualifies its imperatives that violations are "acceptable" if not "right." Thus the delinquent represents not a radical opposition to law-abiding society but something more like an apologetic failure, often more sinned against than sinning in his own eyes. We call these justifications of deviant behavior techniques of neutralization; and we believe these techniques make up a crucial component of Sutherland's "definitions favorable to the violation of law." It is by learning these techniques that the juvenile becomes delinquent, rather than by learning moral imperatives, values or attitudes standing in direct contradiction to those of the dominant society.

Szabo, Denis
Criminology and Crime Policy [72]

The archetype of the delinquent is Cain. The murderer of his brother, he bears the mark of his infamy. The mark of Cain is the commission of the act. From a state of envy, an impulse to attack the material and physical integrity of the other, he actually commits to the act. He kills. An examination of the case of Cain is the first step for the criminologist, and it gives rise to a number of questions at several levels. For the jurist, the act must be intentional. The madman, the psychopath, is irresponsible. He is sick and cannot be a criminal. It is also necessary that the act be a contravention of a clearly established law: that which protects the physical integrity of another. If Abel had threatened Cain, the latter could have called upon the principle of legitimate defense. Also, Cain had a motive: jealousy, envy.

Are Cain's traits, hereditary or acquired, any different from Abel's? His genetic heritage, his anatomy, are they the same as those of his brother? These are the questions that the biologist would ask. The psychologist's question would be, Are Cain's personality and character different, and do they manifest themselves in other traits? Since both are of the same family, both knowing the smile of the same mother and the authority of the same father, can he be the opposite of his brother? The sociologist would want to know the social milieu, the professional standing of the family, its position in society, the physical and moral climate of its surroundings, its culture. Finally,

72 *Criminology and Crime Policy,* trans. Dorothy R. Crelinsten (Lexington, Mass.: Lexington Books, 1979).

human behavior can be observed through the eyes of the state, the political organization, and the socioeconomic system whose laws affect all our lives.

Stimuli of an economic nature are closely involved in many of the motivations for men's actions, and judicial power is one of the functions of the public authority. Here the problems of the political scientist come into play: he would consider Cain in the context of the political organization of the day. Finally, does Abel's life not constitute an absolute value? Does his good fortune, his success, not explain Cain's jealousy? Did he not display this good fortune ostentatiously? Was this good fortune, greater than his brother's, justified? The moralist, too, has a word to say about the criminal.

t

Tarde, Gabriel
Penal Philosophy [73]

If the group of malefactors, which is as variegated as it is numerous, as changing as it is persistent, is not united by a single bond that is truly vital; if there exist between them neither that pathological relationship which a similar form of degeneracy or mental alienation would establish, a same group of maladies with which they would be affected, not that physiological relationship, which their common resemblance to supposed ancestors would bear witness to, of what nature, then, is the bond which brings them together and often gives them a special physiognomy more easily perceived than formulated? In our opinion it is a bond which is entirely social, the intimate relation which is to be observed between people carrying on the same trade or trades of a similar character; and this hypothesis is sufficient to account for even the anatomical peculiarities, especially the physiological and psychological peculiarities by which delinquents are distinguished. Let us first deal with the former.

We have told in a previous chapter why every profession, whether it be open to everybody or enclosed in a caste, must in the long run recruit its members from among those individuals best endowed and best fitted to succeed in it, or develop among its members, through heredity, the talent and, consequently, the forms which

---

73   *Penal Philosophy*, trans. Rapelje Howell (New York: Little, Brown, 1912).

it prefers. This is so not only with regard to every profession, but with regard to every class and every social category that is more or less clearly defined. [...] of all careers, the career of a criminal is indeed the one that is least often entered into by a person having freedom to choose, and is the one where, as a consequence of the rapid extinction of vicious families, the hereditary transmission of aptitudes has less time to be carried out. One has been thrust into it from birth; this is the ordinary case. The majority of murderers and notorious thieves began as children who had been abandoned, and the true seminary of crime must be sought for upon each public square of each crossroad of our towns, whether they be small or large, in those flocks of pillaging street urchins who, like bands of sparrows, associate together, at first for marauding, and then for theft, because of a lack of education and food in their homes. Without any natural predisposition on their part, their fate is often decided by the influence of their comrades. However, there are others whom the fatal logic of their vices has driven to the dilemma of crime or death. And, even with regard to the former, one can say, as a general thing, that the preference which they will give to the example set by a small minority of rascals over the example of the immense majority who are laborious denotes in them some anomaly of nature; although one can reply that it is the same thing with imitation as with attraction which is exercised inversely to the square of the distances. Thus it would be permissible for the child who was the most normally constituted to be more influenced by half a score of perverse friends by whom he is surrounded than by millions of unknown fellow-citizens. In spite of everything, there is no doubt that advancement in the trade of murder or theft ordinarily assumes a true vocation, more or less vaguely recognized by an experienced eye. Also, Topinard and Manouvrier are each separately drawn to this conclusion, that criminals form one of those "professional categories" that we have just been discussing.

[...]

There is not one of even the most precocious of the young monsters of seventeen or eighteen years whose exploits appall the press who has not behind him years of criminal apprenticeship during his entire vagabond and soiled childhood. For the trade of crime, like every other, has its special schools. Also, like every other trade, it has its special idiom, namely, slang. What old and deep-rooted profession has not its own slang, from sailors, masons, and coppersmiths to painters and lawyers,—to the very police agents themselves, who say that they "camoufler" themselves when they mean to "disguise" themselves, and "coton" for a "resemblance," etc.? We can read Maxime du Camp on this subject. Finally, there are special associations, temporary or permanent, epidemic or endemic. As an example of the former, the rising of the peasants in 1358, and in certain respects Jacobinism, which temporarily ravaged France; as an example of the latter, the Camorra and the Maffia, which are traditionally prevalent in Italy. These are great professional syndicates of crime, which have played a far more important historic part than one might suppose. How many times has a warlike band, organized in the very midst of pastoral tribes, been a society of brigands? How many times has this brigandage been the necessary leaven that has served to raise an empire and establish peace through the triumph of the strong?

So, do not reproach me with doing too much honor to crime by placing it among the professions. If the petty criminal industry which languished in the depths of our towns, like so many little shops where a backward manufacture survives, does nothing but harm, the great criminal industry has had its days of great and fearful utility in the past, under its military and despotic form; and, under its financial form, people pretend that it renders appreciable services. Where would we be if there had never been any fortunate criminals, eager to overcome scruples, rights, and customs in order to drive the human race from the pastoral poem to the drama of civilization? And we must not, unfortunately, recognize the fact that from the out and out criminal to the most honest merchant we pass through a series of transitions, that every tradesman who cheats his clients is a thief, that every grocer who adulterates his wine is a poisoner, and that, as a general thing, every man who misrepresents his merchandise is a forger? And I do not mention the great number of industries that exist more or less indirectly through the profits of crime,—low taverns, houses of prostitution, gambling houses, old-clothes shops,—which are just so many places of refuge for the receipt of stolen goods for delinquents. They have many other accomplices. Among the upper classes, how much extortion, how many doubtful bargains, how much traffic in decorations, demand the complicity of people who are rich and reputed to be honest, who profit by them, not always without their knowledge! If the tree of crime, with all its roots and its rootlets, could ever be uprooted from our society, it would leave a giant abyss.

Tarde, Gabriel
The Laws of Imitation[74] *(1890)*

The social like the hypnotic state is only a form of dream, a dream of command and a dream of action. Both the somnambulist and the social man are possessed by the illusion that their ideas, all of which have been suggested to them, are spontaneous.

[...]

What distinguishes us modern Europeans from these alien and primitive societies is the fact that the magnetisation has become mutual, so to speak, at least to a certain extent; and because we, in our democratic pride, a little exaggerate this reciprocity, because, moreover, forgetting that in becoming mutual, this magnetisation, the source of all faith and obedience, has become general, we err in flattering ourselves that we have become less credulous and docile, less imitative, in short, than our ancestors. This is a fallacy, and we shall have to rid ourselves of it. But even if the aforesaid notion were true, it would nevertheless be clear that before the relations of model and copyist, of master and subject, of apostle and neophyte, had become reciprocal or alternative, as we ordinarily see them in our democratic society, they must of necessity have begun by being one-sided and irreversible. Hence castes. Even in the most democratic societies, the one-sidedness and irreversibility in question always exist at the basis of social imitations, i.e. in the family. For the father is and always will be his son's

---

74   *The Laws of Imitation*, trans. Elsie Clews Parsons (New York: Henry Holt and Company, 1903)

first master, priest, and model. Every society, even at present, begins in this way.

Therefore, in the beginning of every old society, there must have been, *a fortiori*, a great display of authority exercised by certain supremely imperious and positive individuals. Did they rule through terror and imposture, as alleged? This explanation is obviously inadequate. They ruled through their *prestige*.

[...]

Mutual imitation, mutual prestige or *sympathy*, in the meaning of Adam Smith, is produced only in our so-called waking life and among people who seem to exercise no magnetic influence over one another.

[...]

Why should we really marvel at the one-sided, passive imitation of the somnambulist? Any act of any one of our fellows inspires us who are lookers-on with the more or less irrational idea of imitation. If we at times resist this tendency, it is because it is neutralised by some antagonistic suggestions of memory or perception. Since the somnambulist is for the time being deprived of this power of resistance, he can illustrate for us the imitative quiescence of the social being in so far as he is social, i.e., in so far as he has relations exclusively with his fellows and, especially, with one of his fellows.

[...]

Thus it is certain that the progress of civilization renders subjection to imitation at once more *personal* and more *rational.* We are just as much enslaved as our ancestors by the examples of our environment, but we make a better use of them through our more logical and more individual choice, one adapted to our own ends and to our particular nature. And yet, as we shall see, this does not keep extra-logical and prestigeful influences from always playing a very considerable part. [...]

Society is imitation, and imitation is a kind of somnambulism.

Thorsten, Sellin
Culture Conflict and Crime[75]

Conflicts of conduct norms may arise in a different manner from that just described. There are social groups on the surface of the earth which possess complexes of conduct norms which, due to differences in the mode of life and the social values evolved by these groups, appear to set them apart from other groups in many or most respects. We may expect conflicts of norms when the rural dweller moves to the city, but we assume that he has absorbed the basic norms of the culture which comprises both town and country. How much greater is not the conflict likely to be when Orient and Occident meet, or when the Corsican mountaineer is transplanted to the lower East Side of New York. Conflicts of cultures are inevitable when the norms of one cultural or subcultural area migrate to come in contact with those of another, and it is interesting to note that most of the specific researches on culture conflict and delinquency have been concerned with this aspect of conflict rather than the one mentioned earlier.

Conflicts between the norms of divergent cultural codes may arise

1. when these codes clash on the border of contiguous culture areas;

2. when, as may be the case with legal norms, the law of one cultural group is extended to cover the territory or another; or

75 *Culture Conflict and Crime* (Brooklyn, NY: Social Science Research Council, 1938).

3. when members of one cultural group migrate to another.

[...]

Culture conflicts are the natural outgrowth of process-es of social differentiation, which produce an infinity of social groupings, each with its own definitions of life situations, its own interpretations of social relations, its own ignorance or misunderstanding of the social values of other groups. The transformation of a culture from a homogeneous and well-integrated type to a heteroge-neous and disinterested type is therefore accompanied by an increase of conflict situations. [...] Such conflicts within a changing culture may be distinguished from those created when different cultural systems come in contact with one another, regardless of the character or stage of development of these systems. In either case, the conduct of members of a group involved in the conflict of codes will in some respects be judged abnormal by the other group.

W

Wilson, James Q.
"Broken Windows"[76]

Philip Zimbardo, a Stanford psychologist, reported in 1969 on some experiments testing the broken-window theory. He arranged to have an automobile without license plates parked with its hood up on a street in the Bronx and a comparable automobile on a street in Palo Alto, California. The car in the Bronx was attacked by "vandals" within ten minutes of its "abandonment." The first to arrive were a family—father, mother, and young son—who removed the radiator and battery. Within twenty-four hours, virtually everything of value had been removed. Then random destruction began—windows were smashed, parts torn off, upholstery ripped. Children began to use the car as a playground. Most of the adult "vandals" were well-dressed, apparently clean-cut whites. The car in Palo Alto sat untouched for more than a week. Then Zimbardo smashed part of it with a sledgehammer. Soon, passersby were joining in. Within a few hours, the car had been turned upside down and utterly destroyed. Again, the "vandals" appeared to be primarily respectable whites.

Untended property becomes fair game for people out for fun or plunder and even for people who ordinarily would not dream of doing such things and who probably consider themselves law-abiding. Because of the

---

76 George L. Kelling and James Q. Wilson, "Broken Windows: The Police and Neighborhood Safety," *The Atlantic,* March 1982.

nature of community life in the Bronx—its anonymity, the frequency with which cars are abandoned and things are stolen or broken, the past experience of "no one caring"—vandalism begins much more quickly than it does in staid Palo Alto, where people have come to believe that private possessions are cared for, and that mischievous behavior is costly. But vandalism can occur anywhere once communal barriers—the sense of mutual regard and the obligations of civility—are lowered by actions that seem to signal that "no one cares."

We suggest that "untended" behavior also leads to the breakdown of community controls. A stable neighborhood of families who care for their homes, mind each other's children, and confidently frown on unwanted intruders can change, in a few years or even a few months, to an inhospitable and frightening jungle. A piece of property is abandoned, weeds grow up, a window is smashed. Adults stop scolding rowdy children; the children, emboldened, become more rowdy. Families move out, unattached adults move in. Teenagers gather in front of the corner store. The merchant asks them to move; they refuse. Fights occur. Litter accumulates. People start drinking in front of the grocery; in time, an inebriate slumps to the sidewalk and is allowed to sleep it off. Pedestrians are approached by panhandlers.

At this point it is not inevitable that serious crime will flourish or violent attacks on strangers will occur. But many residents will think that crime, especially violent crime, is on the rise, and they will modify their behavior accordingly. They will use the streets less often, and when on the streets will stay apart from their fellows, moving with averted eyes, silent lips, and hurried steps.

"Don't get involved." For some residents, this growing atomization will matter little, because the neighborhood is not their "home" but "the place where they live." Their interests are elsewhere; they are cosmopolitans. But it will matter greatly to other people, whose lives derive meaning and satisfaction from local attachments rather than worldly involvement; for them, the neighborhood will cease to exist except for a few reliable friends whom they arrange to meet.

Such an area is vulnerable to criminal invasion. Though it is not inevitable, it is more likely that here, rather than in places where people are confident they can regulate public behavior by informal controls, drugs will change hands, prostitutes will solicit, and cars will be stripped.

ALSO BY THE AUTHOR

The following list details works that the author has written, co-written, or to which he has contributed.

Violences et Insécurité urbaines (Paris: PUF, "Que sais-je?" collection, 1998, 12th edition 2010).

L'Amérique, la violence, le crime (Paris: PUF, 2000, 2nd edition 2001).

La Guerre ne fait que commencer: Réseaux, financements, armements, attentats ... les scénarios de demain (Paris: Éditions JC Lattès, 2002 and Paris: Folio, 2003).

Les Polices en France (Paris: PUF, "Que sais-je?" collection, 2001, 3rd edition 2010).

Le Crime aux États-Unis (Paris, PUF, "Que sais-je?" collection, 2003).

Les Polices aux États-Unis (Paris: PUF, "Que sais-je?" collection, 2003).

"Sûreté et profession." In *Imaginer la sécurité globale,* edited by Jacques-Charles Lemaire and Patrick Laclémence (Brussels: Pensée et Hommes, 2004).

État d'urgence: Réformer ou abdiquer: Le choix français, edited by Roger Fauroux and Bernard Spitz (Paris: Éditions Robert Laffont, 2004).

Deux siècles de débats républicains (Paris: EDIMAF, 2004).

Dico rebelle: Acteurs, lieux, mouvements, edited by Patrick Blaevoet (Paris, Éditions Michalon, 2004).

L'Énigme Al Qaïda (Paris: Éditions JC Lattès, 2005).

Mercenaires et polices privées (Paris: Éditions Universalis, 2006).

Géographie de la France criminelle (Paris: Éditions Odile Jacob, 2006).

Mieux contrôler les fichiers de police pour protéger les libértés (Paris: DocFra, 2008).

World Chaos, Early Detection and Proactive Security (Paris: LASD, 2007).

Vers une plus grande efficacité du service public de sécurité au quotidien (Paris: DocFra, 2008).

L'Année stratégique, 2008-2013 Annuals, DALLOZ 2007-2015

Le Nouveau chaos mondial (Paris: Éditions des Riaux, 2007).

La Criminalité en France (Paris: CNRS Éditions, annual reports, 2007–2012).

Radicalisation en Occident: La Menace Intérieure (New York: NYPD, 2008).

Pour une stratégie globale de sécurité nationale (Paris: Éditions Dalloz, 2008).

Vidéosurveillance et vidéoprotection (Paris: PUF, "Que sais-je?" collection, 2008, 2nd edition 2012).

Terrorism Early Warning: 10 Years of Achievement in Fighting Terrorism and Crime (Los Angeles: LASD, 2008).

Le 11 septembre (Mémorial de Caen—*Ouest France,* 2008).

Football et société (Paris: Fédération française de football, 2008).

100 mots pour comprendre l'actualité (Paris: PUF, 2008).

Jeux en lignes et menace criminelle (Paris: DocFra, 2008).

Les 100 mots de la police et du crime (Paris: PUF, "Que sais-je?" collection, 2009).

Les Études de sécurité publique (Paris: PUF, "Que sais-je?" collection, 2009).

Les Fichiers de police et de gendarmerie (Paris: PUF, "Que sais-je ?" collection, 2009, 2nd edition 2011).

La Face noire de la mondialisation (Paris: CNRS Éditions, 2009).

Mieux contrôler les fichiers de police (Paris: DocFra, 2009)

Les Terroristes disent toujours ce qu'ils vont faire (Paris: PUF, 2010).

À La recherche de la criminologie (Paris: CNRS Éditions, 2010).

Les 100 mots du terrorisme (Paris: PUF, "Que sais-je?" collection, 2010).

Criminologie plurielle (Paris: PUF, 2010).

Statistiques criminelles et enquêtes de victimation (Paris: PUF, "Que sais-je?" collection, 2011).

Les Politiques publiques de sécurité (Paris: PUF, "Que sais-je?" collection, 2011).

Les Fichiers de police et de gendarmerie, une nouvelle étape vers une nécessaire transparence (Paris: DocFra, 2011).

Livre Blanc sur la sécurité publique (Paris: DocFra, 2011).

Une Histoire criminelle de la France (Paris: Éditions Odile Jacob, 2012, paperback 2013).

Dictionnaire amoureux du crime (Paris: Éditions Plon, 2013).

La Criminologie pour les nuls (Paris: Éditions First, 2012).

Dernières nouvelles du crime (Paris: CNRS Éditions, 2013, translated into Italian, English, and Chinese).

Le Terrorisme pour les nuls (Paris: Éditions First, 2014)

Une Histoire de la médecine légale et de l'Anthropologie criminelle (Paris: PUF, 2015).

Terrorismes (Paris: Éditions Dalloz, 2015).

Qui est l'ennemi? (Paris: CNRS Éditions, 2015, translated into Italian, English, and Chinese).